PRESENTED TO:

_____

FROM:

_____

DATE:

_____

PLAN A *happy* LIFE™

PLAN A

happy

LIFE™

DEFINE YOUR PASSION, NURTURE YOUR
CREATIVITY, AND TAKE HOLD OF YOUR DREAMS

STEPHANIE FLEMING

THOMAS NELSON
Since 1798

Published in Nashville, Tennessee, by Thomas Nelson. Thomas Nelson is a registered trademark of HarperCollins Christian Publishing, Inc.

Photos by The Happy Planner.

Thomas Nelson titles may be purchased in bulk for educational, business, fund-raising, or sales promotional use. For information, please e-mail SpecialMarkets@ThomasNelson.com.

ISBN 978-1-4041-1469-2 (custom)
ISBN 978-1-4002-1689-5

Printed in China

20 21 22 23 24   WAI   10 9 8 7 6 5 4 3 2 1

TO KEVIN.

THANK YOU FOR

BELIEVING IN ME.

I LOVE YOU THE MOST!

contents

IV. LIVING HAPPY

introduction

Stop asking for permission to be happy.
Create your own happiness!

Back in 1998, my whole life was changed by a conversation at a baseball game, though I didn't realize it at the time. My mom and I had a vision to create stickers specifically designed for the newly emerging craft of scrapbooking. We had each reached a point in our lives where something really needed to change. So we took a huge leap of faith and started our company: me & my BIG ideas—mambi for short   because dreaming up *big* ideas is our specialty!

After lots of hard work, some successes, and some failures, our little garage-based business has grown into an industry-leading brand that seeks to inspire our customers to *live creatively*. In the spring of 2015, we launched the Happy Planner, and it has quickly become the most popular and best-selling product line in our company's twenty-year history. And while all that is wonderful, the greatest blessing has been to

see the difference our products are making in the lives of so many. Our brand's messages—Live Creatively® and Plan a Happy Life™—are so much more than words to me. I strive, as an individual and a company, to encourage others to explore their own creativity as a path to the happy life they are seeking.

Living creatively has truly become a way of life for me now, and for that I am so very grateful. It's really been an amazing story, but at the end of the day—and at the beginning and in every moment in the middle—I'm a real person, just like you. I've faced some difficult things in my life. Some really, really hard things. I've been scared and sad, angry and hurt. I've battled depression and lived in denial. I've agonized over a broken heart, a broken marriage, and bills I had no idea how I was going to pay. This whole mambi dream began with a desire to earn money, yes, but more than that, to figure out a way to live this life on my own terms, to finally be in control of creating my own happiness.

LIVING CREATIVELY HAS TRULY BECOME A WAY OF LIFE FOR ME.

And I've done it. I've found the happy life I was searching for. Not perfect, not sunshine every moment, but *happy* at its foundation. Now I want to help you find your happy life too. I call it the Happy Life Movement.

I'm not going to pretend I have all the answers. I'm not here to tell you step-by-step how to have a happy life—or even what your happy life should look like. But I am a student of life, learning as I go. And I have all these experiences and the lessons I've learned through those experiences. I want to share with you the tools that have worked for me, that have helped me claim the happy life I want to live.

The last thing I want to do is be yet another "I have all the answers" person. I'm offering you tools, not prescriptions. There is no one-system-fits-all. So if you've been looking for permission to ditch the self-help "expert" and carve out your own path to happiness and to the life you want to live . . . here it is. Figure out what works for you. Do it, and be happy!

> I'M OFFERING YOU TOOLS, NOT PRESCRIPTIONS. THERE IS NO ONE-SYSTEM-FITS-ALL.

Plan a Happy Life isn't about doing life *my* way. It's about defining what happiness looks like for *you*. It's about harnessing the power of planning and unleashing your own innate creativity to carve out and claim your own happy life. And it's about enabling and encouraging everyone around you to do the same.

Will planning guarantee you happiness, that you'll never have another sad moment or struggle? Of course not. That's just not reality. Life isn't an Instagram feed. Planning will, however, enable you to define what you want, take hold of your dreams, and actively seek to make them come true.

In these pages, you'll not only find the tips and strategies that work for me, but you'll also find my hopes, my dreams, and my prayers for you. Because above all, I want you to be brave with your life. Don't be afraid to try something new, to be less than perfect, even to fail sometimes. Don't be afraid to be you. Because you *can* do this . . . you can *Plan a Happy Life*!

MY GOAL, MY *true mission,*

IS TO SPREAD HAPPY

WHEREVER I GO AND TO

INSPIRE AND ENABLE

WOMEN EVERYWHERE TO

embrace the positive

AND CLAIM THE HAPPY

LIFE THEY WANT TO LIVE.

Stephanie

PART I

DEFINING HAPPY

BE *brave* WITH YOUR LIFE!

CHAPTER 1

Creativity is the song of your imagination. Sing your song!

You may be asking yourself, Why is the first chapter in this book on *happiness* about creativity? That's a great question! I believe that creativity is essential to living a happy life. In fact, I believe it's where the journey to joy and happiness begins.

What is creativity? Forget everything you've been taught. We're going to start from scratch. In its truest sense, creativity is your imagination in action. Think of it this way: *imagination* is what happens in your head; it's the dreams you dream. *Creativity*, then, is what happens when you dare to do something with those imaginative ideas. When you bring them out into the world. And it isn't limited to the arts, as many of us are conditioned to believe. It's for all of us who dare to put our imaginations to work. It's for *you*. From building a new car to solving a problem in a way no one else has thought of—that's creativity. It happens every day, all around you, and in ways you might not typically think of as being creative.

I believe we are *all* creative beings. We just are. Inside each and every one of us—and yes, that means you too—there is this innate ability that drives us to create something from nothing. That something can be an object, an idea, a solution, or a song. Whatever *it* is, it was created by *you*. You were created to create! To share your unique gifts and talents with the world. Expressing ourselves creatively helps us define our purpose, and *that* is the first step in planning a happy life.

Does the thought of defining your purpose intimidate you? Fear not. You are not alone! If you asked me what my purpose was ten years ago, I wouldn't have been able to give you an answer. In fact, I wouldn't have been able to tell you what my unique talents and gifts were . . . or what made me happy (beyond my love for my children). I had some work to do, and I did it. I dove deep into learning about *who* I was and *what* I wanted to do in life. I gave life to the ideas floating around in this big ol' melon of mine; and trust me, there's a *lot* of space for ideas. I learned so much about myself and the process of living creatively. That is what I want for you too. Keep reading, and we'll walk through some helpful exercises to get you on your way to living creatively!

NURTURING MY *creativity* IS WHAT KEEPS ME GOING. IT'S WHAT FUELS MY FIRE. IT'S MY *passion* IN LIFE. IT'S THE WAY THAT I EXPRESS MYSELF AND THE WAY THAT I FEEL LIKE I CAN BE SEEN IN THE WORLD.

Stephanie

NURTURING YOUR CREATIVITY

Let's talk about the concept of nurturing your creativity. It is true that there are times when creativity just happens, when it just pours out of a person in breathtaking ways. More often, though, creativity is at first a fragile thing that needs to be nurtured, fed, and gently encouraged to grow. But the wonderful thing is, the more we nurture and encourage our own creativity, the less fragile it becomes. Over time we become conditioned to think and respond and, yes, even live creatively. There's no need to limit creativity to specific projects or areas of our lives. We can create simply for the joy of creating.

One of the best ways to nurture that creative spark that lives within each of us is to challenge ourselves to try something new. What is something you have always wanted to try? Maybe it's hand lettering, or cooking with a wok, or learning how to write software. Give it a try! See what you like about it and what you don't like about it. And then . . .

GIVE YOURSELF PERMISSION TO FAIL

Yes, you read that right. *Give yourself permission to fail.* Failing doesn't make you a failure. That's a statement worth repeating. *Failing doesn't make you a failure.* We need to change the perception of what failure is. Because, in fact, failing is a huge part of the way we learn.

➤ If you try something, and it doesn't turn out perfectly the first time, that doesn't make you a failure.

➤ If you try something and decide you don't like it, that doesn't make you a failure.

➤ If you try something and simply aren't good at it, you aren't a failure either.

Allow yourself to be less than perfect. Express your creativity, and *let it be okay* if whatever you've tried doesn't come out exactly the way you thought it should.

So often, the thing that holds us back from being truly creative is fear. Fear of being judged, fear of not being good enough, fear of not being able to fulfill what you say you want to do, fear of . . . well . . . just lots of fear. If you are going to be creative, you can't be afraid of failure or judgment. You've got to just let yourself *be* creative. If that means you never show another living soul what you've created, that is okay. Do it just for you. Write because you like to write. Create something in your planner and play with stickers because you enjoy it. Paint simply because you like the feeling of putting paint on canvas. It doesn't have to hang in anybody's home. If it makes you feel whole and happy, do it!

SO OFTEN, THE THING THAT HOLDS US BACK FROM BEING TRULY CREATIVE IS FEAR.

Stop looking at the pieces that aren't perfect, and look at what you've done that makes you happy. Embrace the imperfections! After all, they

PART OF THE BEAUTY
AND WONDER OF
CREATIVITY IS THE VERY FACT
THAT IT CAN BE EXPRESSED
SO UNIQUELY!

are a part of what makes you wonderfully you. Remember, trying *is* success in the creative space.

WHAT'S YOUR PASSION?

So how do you want to express your creativity? What is it that you most want to do? In other words, what's your passion? If you can't name a specific thing, don't worry. Lots of people aren't sure what their passion is. Try thinking of it this way: If you were left alone for a week—with no work, no distractions, no responsibilities—what would you do? What is that thing you could get lost in for a whole week? That thing that would have you jumping out of bed in the morning and staying up far too late at night? *That's* your passion.

EVERYDAY CREATIVITY

Creativity doesn't have to be huge. Here are some simple ideas for tapping into your creative spirit:

➤ Doodle . . . with lots of different colors.
➤ Keep a notebook to jot down all your big ideas.
➤ Try a new recipe.
➤ Figure out a more scenic route to work or school.
➤ Sing out loud in the car or in the shower.

If you still aren't sure what your passion is, try a few different things. Soon enough you'll stumble on something that causes a revolution in your heart and makes your soul sing. And it might not be what the world traditionally considers creative. There is always a creative side to those things you are passionate about. For example, if you have a passion for helping people, chances are your creativity is expressed in the ways you help. Perhaps you cook for the homeless, organize fundraisers, or gather flowers to share from your garden. Those are creative expressions. You are creating something that wasn't there before, something to help someone else. Part of the beauty and wonder of creativity is the very fact that it can be expressed so uniquely!

Creating simply for the joy of creating helps you define what you want, who you are, what makes you tick. Which in turn leads to your passion.

LIVE CREATIVELY EVERY DAY

Okay, admit it: you *love* being creative. Or then again, maybe you aren't sure about this whole creativity thing, but you'd like to give it a try. It's tough to carve out those days, those hours to devote to your creative pursuits. So let's figure out how to live creatively in the any-day, everyday moments of your life. We all know it's not something that's just going to happen by itself. It takes determination. It takes intentionality. It takes *planning*.

A NOTE FROM TERRI GICK, MY MOM AND COFOUNDER OF ME & MY BIG IDEAS

To me, living creatively means having the ability to play and experiment with things that interest you and arrange them in new and different ways that may not be conventional. Risking the sting of judgment and being creative feeds the soul in a very nurturing way for me. It's a form of play that keeps my heart and mind healthy and happy. I have built a life around living creatively. It keeps me engaged in the process of life, and it brings me great joy. As an added bonus, I've been able to use creativity throughout my career working with designers and artists to do some pretty cool things.

For as long as I can remember, I have had multiple creative projects going on at the same time. When I get bored with knitting, I move into the garden! When I have the first coat of paint on the canvas in the garage, I move into the kitchen and arrange some flowers. I might rearrange the accessories on the coffee table as I pass through the living room. Through the years I have tried my hand at crochet, knitting, gardening, painting, cross-stitch, macramé, candle making, floral arranging, stained glass, scrapbooking, sandblasting, quilting, jewelry making, pottery, sewing, photography, decorating, and T-shirt painting . . . to name a few of my skills!

As I sit here writing this, I am wrapping up one of the most creative projects ever!

Two years ago, I was at a place in my life where I felt the deep need for a creative project, something *big*, something *fun*, something *different*. So I bought an older one-story home thinking a

remodel would fill my need to create. My vision was to build a sanctuary-like space where I could live the rest of my life.

I wanted it to be peaceful and calming with lots of nature everywhere and room to wander. I wanted the space to speak to me. Everyone thought I was crazy to turn this five-bedroom home into a two-bedroom home, but it works for me and I love it! Maybe it's not good for resale, but hey, I just built my forever home, and I'm living creatively every day here. Most importantly, I had fun doing this, I am proud of it, and I love the feeling I get living here. I'm grateful and blessed. (I'm also looking for another creative project!)

I believe creativity is essential to a happy, healthy, productive life. Make room in your life for whatever it is that brings you joy, sets your soul on fire, and makes you happy. Take the creativity within you, that desire to take something that lives in your dreams—whether it's a book or a meal, a software program or a new kind of car—and dare to bring it out into the world. Dare to live creatively!

IMAGINE, DREAM, CREATE

If you had an hour, a whole day, an entire week to yourself, what would you do? What would make your soul sing?

DARE
TO LIVE
CREATIVELY!

➤ An hour

➤ A day

➤ A week

NEW FOR YOU

One of the greatest ways to nurture your creativity is to try something new. It can be anything, really—from something big, like skydiving or learning to paint with watercolors, to something not quite so big, like journaling a bit every day or rearranging a room. It might be something just for you or something that helps others. Your "something new" can even be as simple as trying a new recipe or arranging a vase of flowers. You just might discover your lifelong passion or simply a pleasant way to while away an hour or two. Just jump in and see if it sparks a fire inside you. What are some new things you would like to try?

➤ Big things:

➤ Little things:

➤ In-between things:

➤ "For me" things:

➤ "For others" things:

FOR ME, BEING IN THE BEAUTY OF *nature* NOT ONLY SPARKS MY CREATIVITY, BUT IT ALSO HELPS ME REFOCUS MY LIFE AND MY PRIORITIES. IN THE MOUNTAINS, AMONG THE TREES, LAKES, AND FRESH AIR, I AM ABLE TO *calm* MY BUSY MIND AND EASE MY ANXIETIES. STEPPING OUTSIDE ALLOWS CREATIVITY TO STEP IN.

Stephanie

MOVED BY THE MUSIC

In her book *Emma*, Jane Austen wrote, "Without music, life would be a blank to me." What does music write on the pages of your life? What songs or styles of music make you feel

- ➤ creative?
- ➤ peaceful?
- ➤ inspired?
- ➤ energized?
- ➤ ready to change the world—or at least your place in it?

Create a playlist that gets your creativity flowing.

LOOK AND SEE

Doing isn't the only way to nurture your creativity. Whether it's DIY, fiction, or nonfiction, reading and even watching movies and television shows can also spark your more imaginative side.

- ➤ What books and authors inspire you?
- ➤ List some books (or some authors) you've been wanting to read.
- ➤ What are some movies and shows that inspire you?
- ➤ List some movies and shows you would like to see.

GIVE IT A TRY!

➤ Paint something: a picture, a table, or even a wall.

➤ Write something: a story, a poem, or simply your thoughts.

➤ Decorate something: your desk, a table, or a room.

➤ Go outside and see what you can see.

➤ Read, watch, or listen to something that inspires you.

➤ Help someone.

A GOAL
WITHOUT
A PLAN
IS JUST A
WISH.

happy to be you

You were not born to be perfect.
You were born to be real.

You are enough. Do you believe that? That you—just as you are, right this moment—are enough. Because the first step to planning a happy life isn't really a step at all; it's a pause. It's taking the time to stand in your own presence and say, *I am enough, just the way I am. I am worthy.*

This doesn't have anything to do with vanity or arrogance. It's not denying or taking anything away from anyone else's worth. It's simply recognizing that you yourself are an amazing creation. And that you are worthy of all the love and happiness this life has to offer. We're going for confidence, not conceit.

There was a time, just a few years ago, when I didn't believe those things about myself. I wanted desperately to feel confident and happy; instead, I was filled with self-doubt, and my self-esteem was at zero. I was stuck in an abusive and unhappy marriage. Not only did I not feel happy in my life, I didn't feel happy in myself. But I began to make changes.

I began to work on getting to know myself. I embraced the things I was proud of and changed the things I wanted to improve. And I actually began to feel confident and happy. Because I was choosing who I wanted me to be. It took me five years from my first separation until the official divorce. And while that whole experience brought me to my knees and almost broke me, it didn't. I came out on the other side stronger than I had been before.

When we don't believe we are worthy, that we are enough—just as we are today, right in this moment—then it doesn't matter how perfect the rest of our lives are. Happiness will always be just out of reach. But when we believe we are worthy of love, success, health, and, yes, happiness—then it is possible to find happiness, no matter how imperfect our lives are.

Do you believe you are worthy, that you are enough just as you are? Do you deserve to be happy?

You need to be able to stand in your own presence and say, "My life might be a hot mess right now, but I really like who I am. And no matter where I am in my life, I am worthy of love. I am worthy of all the happiness this life has to offer. Yes, I have some things I can improve, and that's okay because everyone does."

Believing you are enough isn't believing you are perfect. No one gets to claim that. We've all made mistakes, but we don't have to allow them to define us. And we all have things we want to change about ourselves, but our goals for ourselves and our lives are not a reflection on our value or worth. They're part of who we are and who we want to become.

So let's stop and think for a moment. Assess where you are today and who you choose to be.

I believe I am

loved
_____

I believe I am

_____

I believe I am

_____

When we set out to make changes in our lives, it can't be because we're trying to be more worthy, to become more loved, or to gain attention. Because if that's our reasoning, any change we try to make will fall short. Actively pursue the things that make you happy—not to be more worthy, but because you already are.

LEARNING TO LOVE YOURSELF

Once we decide that we are enough, that we are worthy of claiming our own happy life, the next step is to learn to radically love ourselves. Just as we are—right this very moment. Because we can't truly invite happiness and success into our lives until we do. Period. No "whens" or "ifs" attached. You know what I'm talking about: "When I lose weight . . ." "If I make more money . . ." "When I'm in a relationship . . ." "If I get the job . . ." Get rid of those qualifiers. You don't need them. Love yourself right now, just as you are.

THINK ON THIS

What are the "whens" and "ifs" you have in your life?

_____

Write out a commitment today to get rid of those qualifiers.

_____

WORDS HAVE POWER

Words have power, especially the words we say to ourselves. If we truly want to learn to love ourselves and claim the happy life we want to live, it's crucial that we create a positive narrative in our own minds about who we are. We have to be our own biggest cheerleaders.

GIVE IT A TRY

These days I'm a sucker for a cheesy selfie.

I spent so many years not feeling comfortable on the receiving side of the camera lens. Now that I've learned to love myself for who I am, just as I am, I love selfies! They are my way of saying, "I was here, living and loving life!" Selfies remind me that I'm worthy of being seen, no matter what I look like. And so are you! So take a cheesy selfie today. Show the world you are here . . . living and loving life. Be seen!

Yet so often the reality is that we are our own biggest critics. And believe me, I know what I'm talking about here. For years I have struggled with my body image. My own personal battle to love myself becomes really evident in the way I think about my body and the way I talk to myself about my body.

There was a time when I would look in the mirror, and the dialogue would go something like this: "Look at that stomach. You are so fat!" Not anymore. One of the things I've learned is that loving myself includes loving and taking care of my body. I've worked hard to change the dialogue that goes on in my head when I look in the

mirror. And over time, "You're so fat" has become "Thank you, strong and beautiful body, for helping me bring two healthy children into the world and for taking care of me even when I didn't always take care of you."

I challenge you to look in the mirror every day and give yourself at least one sincere compliment. Decide to celebrate and honor all that you are instead of dwelling on everything you believe you should be but think you aren't. I promise you, this really works. In fact, I use positive affirmations every day, throughout the day, to remind myself that I am enough, that I am worthy, that I am loved by me. I put notes on the mirror, stickers in my planner, and notes in my car. I even write the occasional letter to myself.

GIVE IT A TRY

Write at least one sincere compliment to yourself and stick it on the bathroom mirror. Yep, right there where you can't deny it.

Maybe that sounds too simple. Maybe it even sounds a bit silly. But the fact is, when I changed the way I talked to myself, things began to change in my life. They really did. I disassociated my self-worth from that number on the scale. And yes, being completely honest, I am still working on this—it really is a lifelong journey—but I see myself differently now, and that has made all the difference. (And here's a bonus benefit: once I learned to honor the body I have been blessed with, it became so much easier to take care of it.)

Be kind to yourself. The journey of life can be tough. We don't need our inner critic throwing rotten tomatoes at us along the way. Loving yourself *and* being loving to yourself are so important if you want to make changes in your life. Believe you are worthy of love, success, health, and happiness—and then tell yourself you are.

DON'T BE AFRAID TO BE YOU

I'll admit it: confidence has not come easy for me. For years I hid behind my insecurities, fearing that if people saw the real, imperfect me they would turn away. Now I realize those fears caused me to miss out on so much joy and so many experiences. So a few years back, after learning to truly love myself, I decided to ditch all that and live life out loud! No more hiding. No more doubting. Today I know that I am whole and worthy just as I am.

I wish I had learned this lesson earlier in life, but now that I have, I want to encourage you to let go of your fears too. Don't be afraid to be yourself. You have a uniqueness that only you can share with the world.

BE BRIGHT.
BE HAPPY.
BE YOU!

C'mon, don't hold out on us! You do *you*! Embrace your authenticity and individuality. You are enough. You can have a full and purpose-filled life. Don't settle for anything less. (And by the way, it's okay if this isn't an overnight thing. Small steps are still forward steps!)

GIVE IT A TRY

Want to feel more confident? Try this simple exercise: write down one thing about yourself that you love and then claim it every single day. Speak it. Write it. Own it. *Unapologetically.* And don't worry; it's not boastful or conceited to believe in and love yourself. You are enough and can have a full and purpose-filled life. Don't settle for anything less.

_____

_____

RUN YOUR OWN RACE

We are, each of us, running our own race. It took me years to figure that out. I can't tell you how much of my life I wasted comparing myself to those I thought had it better or easier than I did. Picking up my kids from school was the worst! I looked at all the other moms and compared myself to all of them. She was younger, older, thinner, prettier, had more money, a happier marriage, bigger house . . . the list went on and on. It wasn't until I did some deep soul searching that I decided to let all that comparison nonsense go. It's exhausting and unproductive. At best, it leaves us feeling inadequate, and at worst, unworthy.

Let's be real: none of us is perfect. All that per-fection you see on social media is not reality. It's someone's highlight reel. Possibly photoshopped and definitely staged. Nobody has it perfectly all together all the time. And who said we couldn't be wonderfully worthy in the midst of all our imperfections? Real is beautiful, and so are you.

REAL IS BEAUTIFUL!

You are a work in progress, a masterpiece in the making. Resist the urge to compare yourself to others. This life is a journey of trial and error. As long as you keep moving forward and growing each day, that's what matters.

Comparison is a thief that steals our confidence and joy.

Don't miss out on life's adventures because you don't feel perfect. Love yourself. No matter where you are in the journey. And don't let another minute of life pass you by. Soak it all up. Feel the joy every day! You are worth it!

GIVE IT A TRY

Guess what? The best way to silence the comparison creep is self-confidence. You can be a work in progress and still love who you are. Jot down a few sentences declaring your perfectly imperfect place in this world! For example: I am a working mom who deeply loves her children. I am proud of my career and am a present and nurturing mother, wife, and friend!

These are your power statements and should be used any time you feel insecure or less-than. Try finding your own!

_____

_____

_____

▲

Sometimes I worry that people look at me and see only the "success story." That's why I believe it's important to share the reality too. Just hearing the highlights oversimplifies the process and leaves out the valuable lessons I've learned—and am still learning—on my journey as a creative entrepreneur and as a woman. More importantly, it can lead others to believe that their struggles and challenges must mean they're doing something wrong.

The truth is, this life is hard. But don't let your past, your mistakes, or even your failures define you. Because this life, with all its ups and downs, is a beautiful blessing. Make it your own. Define your happy life. Plan for it. And claim it for yourself.

Yes, I am an optimist. And sometimes people confuse optimism with being delusional or fake, pretending to be happy even when things are terrible. But I believe in realistic optimism, acknowledging challenges and then bravely proceeding with positivity, faith, and hope.

Sometimes we all need this reminder: you have the power to own your story. You don't have to prove anything to anyone but yourself. Do you like who you are? If you do, that is all that matters. If you don't, make some changes. And always start with these truths: You are enough. You are worthy. You are lovable.

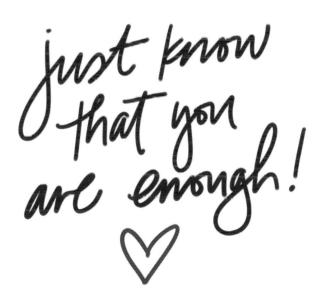

Write a letter to yourself. Fill it with encouragement, kind words, and love.

GIVE IT A TRY

Dear _____,

_____

_____

_____

_____

_____

_____

_____

Love, _____

CHAPTER 3

finding your happy

Be original. Be authentic. Be you!

Someone once asked me to define *happiness*, but that's not really something I feel comfortable doing—at least not for anyone other than myself. Happiness is so different for each of us. We each have to take the time and do the work to figure out what our own happiness is. Your happy life isn't going to be the same as mine. And it sure isn't going to look like all those carefully curated snapshots of life on Instagram or Pinterest.

Before you can create happiness in your own life, you have to define what it means to you. Figuring out what makes you happy will help you define who

HAPPINESS IS SO DIFFERENT FOR EACH OF US.

you are, what you want, and what makes you tick . . . and will ultimately lead you to your passion and purpose in life.

HAPPINESS IS NOT . . .

Happiness is not perfection, and perfection is not happiness.

Let's all drop the masks and be real with each other. Because isn't the struggle to keep up the charade of perfection a huge part of the cause of our unhappiness? The truth is, none of us is perfect and none of us has a perfect life—certainly not me. *But I am happy in my life.* That's a truth worth repeating. I am not perfect, I don't have a perfect life, but I am happy.

> HAPPINESS IS NOT PERFECTION, AND PERFECTION IS NOT HAPPINESS.

And I want you to know that if I can be imperfect and happy, so can you. You don't have to wait for your life to be perfect in order to be happy. When we have the courage to stop pretending to be perfect and let those around us see that we are happy in spite of—or maybe even because of—the imperfections, then we can give others the courage to be happy too.

THINK ON THIS

Are there areas in your life you are holding out for perfection?

_____

_____

How could holding out for perfection steal your happiness?

_____

_____

_____

FINDING YOUR OWN HAPPINESS

What is _your_ definition of happiness? How do you define it for yourself? It really comes down to answering these two big-picture questions for yourself:

Who do you want to be?
What do you want to do?

The key to living a happy life is identifying the answers to these two questions and then making intentional plans to bring those things into your life. Because once you've identified who you want to be and what you want to do, it becomes much easier to make decisions, set goals, and create a plan to make your *who* and *what* a reality.

So let's figure out your *who* and *what*. Grab a piece of paper and start writing. List all the things that make you happy, bring you joy, and make you smile. Big things, little things, silly things, and seemingly impossible things. Don't edit yourself. This is *your* list, and no one else ever has to see it. Here are some prompts to get the ball rolling:

Who do you want to be?

What do you like most about yourself?

_____

_____

Are there things you'd like to change about yourself or areas you'd like to grow in?

_____

_____

_____

What would you most like to be known and remembered for?

_____

_____

What kind of relationship do you want to have with yourself, with others, with your faith?

_____

_____

_____

_____

_____

What do you want to do?

What do you want to accomplish in your personal and business life?

_____

_____

PLAN A *happy* LIFE

_____

_____

What sort of activities do you want to be sure to include in your life?

_____

_____

_____

_____

Are there new things you'd like to try? Or things you'd like to bring back into your life?

_____

_____

_____

_____

44

What are the things you have strong opinions about, the things you really believe in?

_____

_____

_____

_____

What could you talk about for hours?

_____

_____

_____

_____

Again, don't worry about perfection, and don't overthink this. It doesn't have to be neat or all in a row. Just write. Circle, connect with arrows, and highlight with stars. Jot down everything that pops into your mind. The time for analyzing will come

DO WHAT MAKES YOUR SOUL SHINE!

later. And don't rush this process. It probably won't happen overnight, but it will guide your mind to focus on what really matters. Write what you can now, and then set it aside. Over the next few days, add anything else you might think of. As the list grows, see if anything pops off the page. Explore it all.

As you fill in your page (or pages), you might start to wonder how you can be sure that these answers are genuinely your "happy" and not someone else's. (Any other people pleasers out there?) It's really quite easy. Just like in elementary school, keep your eyes on your own paper and don't compare your life with anyone else's. Ask yourself: Are these the things that fill me with profound joy and a sense of real purpose? If you answered yes, you're on to something. Keep walking down this path and periodically check in with yourself to make sure you're still following your own map to happiness and not someone else's.

> DANCE TO THE BEAT OF YOUR OWN DRUMMER, AND DON'T CARE WHAT ANYONE ELSE THINKS OF YOUR CHOREOGRAPHY.

And don't be afraid to cross something off your list if you realize it doesn't really fit your definition of happiness. Do what you need to do to feel complete. Dance to the beat of your own drummer, and don't care what anyone else thinks of your choreography.

THE NEXT STEP

Once you've got your list filled in, sit down and try to capture it in two big-picture mission statements for your life. The first should answer the question of who you want to be and the second of what you want to do. For me, the answers play out in my life like this:

Who do I want to be?
I want to be healthy, happy, kind and compassionate, and a loving and active part of my family's life.

What do I want to do?

I want to pursue my business goals with integrity and passion and to always nurture my creativity.

Note that these answers will likely change over the course of your life. Different seasons call for different dreams, goals, and plans. This isn't something you're going to carve in stone. Just answer for this moment in your life. And when you need to adjust . . . adjust.

THINK ON THIS

Who I want to be:

_____

_____

_____

_____

_____

HAPPINESS IS NOT
THE ABSENCE OF
STRUGGLE. IT'S HOW
YOU FACE THE BAD
TIMES AND THE
positive times.

Stephanie

What I want to do:

_____

_____

_____

_____

_____

OBSTACLES TO OVERCOME

Now I want you to think about this question: What obstacles will make it challenging to live your happiest life? Because as you look at what a happy life means to you, you must also take stock of the obstacles standing in the way of your happiness.

I'll start. Two things really challenge me, and I have to focus on keeping them in check *daily*. The first is managing the balance between my work and my personal life. It's so easy for that to get off-kilter.

LOVE YOUR LIFE; AND IF YOU DON'T, CHANGE IT!

And the second is keeping my insecurities in check, in particular my worries over body image and my struggle to love and accept myself.

Just as you did with your *who* and *what*, make a list of your obstacles. Don't overthink them and don't let them overwhelm you. Just make a realistic and honest list, and then keep it with your *who* and *what* statements. We're going to deal with those guys in a later chapter on planning. But the first step to overcoming these obstacles is to acknowledge them and call them by name.

THINK ON THIS

Obstacles to overcome:

_____

_____

_____

_____

▲

A happy life is not a destination we suddenly arrive at one day and—*poof!*—the journey is over. *Congratulations, you're now happy!* That just doesn't happen. If we want a happy life, we have to have the courage and the determination to create it for ourselves. It's something we'll have to seek out and work at every day. Some days will be easier than others.

Right now you're probably still figuring out what happy looks like for you. And that's so okay—you don't have to have it all figured out. Just start. The change will feel awkward and uncomfortable at first. But hang in there, keep on keeping on, and it will start to feel natural.

You've got this, my friend.

GIVE IT A TRY

Create Your Own Vision Board

A vision board is a creative way to define your happy life. Much like an old-fashioned collage, it visually captures not only those things that bring you joy but also the goals you have for your life. But creating a vision board is about more than just cutting stuff out and putting it together. It's a powerful tool that defines what you really want in life and then physically puts it down in a visually appealing way that you'll want to look at every day. A vision board says, *Hey! This is what you want. See these things right here, right in front of your face? These are the things you've said you want and that you think are important in your life.* Your vision board isn't necessarily something for anyone else to look at. It can be, but it doesn't have to be. It can be just for you.

Your personal vision board will be a daily reminder of your purpose, of how creative you are, and of what you want your life to look like going forward. It will enable you to be intentional about the direction of your life, and it will empower your decision-making by keeping your goals front and center. So let's get started with your vision for your life.

1. First, grab a pen and some paper, and define some of your goals. These can be goals for the coming year or the coming season of your life. Or you can dream big and define your life's goals. What is it that you want? What are the things that will make you happy? Make a list of those things. Do you want to quit your job and work for yourself? That's a goal; write that down. Do you want to spend more time outdoors? Write that down. What do you want your life to look like?
2. Decide what kind of vision board you want to create. Will it be a smaller size to fit inside your daily planner? Will it be on a poster board to hang on a wall? Or perhaps you want to put it on a canvas for a bigger, sturdier vision board.
3. Next, find a way to capture and express your goals visually. For many, that means pictures; but for others it's more

about the words. Somehow find a way to represent what you want. For example, if you want to be with your family more, grab a family picture to put front and center. Cut out words, phrases, and inspirational sayings. Go on Pinterest. Look through magazines. Use your own photos.

4. Now it's time to assemble everything. Group your photos and sayings according to the goal they represent. Arrange them on the surface you've chosen, and begin gluing them down. You can use a roller-type adhesive to attach them to paper, a glue stick for poster board, or a decoupage glue for a canvas.

5. Place your vision board wherever you'll see it daily and be inspired.

Favorite Vision Board Sayings

➤ Happy and healthy.

➤ I can and I will.

➤ Live creatively!

➤ You've got this.

➤ Gratitude changes everything.

Goals from Stephanie's Vision Board

➤ Continue my healthy journey.

➤ Encourage and empower others by connecting in the community.

➤ Nurture my creativity.
➤ Focus and slow down.
➤ Simplify and declutter.

PURPOSE

PLANNING

POSITIVITY

PERSISTENCE

A *happy* LIFE

PART II

THE FOUR Ps

CHAPTER 4

purpose

Happiness is living on
purpose and with purpose.

Now you've done some work figuring out who you are and who you want to be. You have some ideas about how you want your happy life to look. And you know you are worthy of going after it. So what's next?

It's time to take those two big-picture mission statements you created in the last chapter and refine them down to a specific purpose with specific goals.

Decide specifically what you want to accomplish to move forward in your journey to be who you want to be and do what you want to do. This will become your purpose, your intention, your focus. Call it whatever you want to call it; just be sure to *define it* and *write it down.* Because without a purpose in mind—without a sense of direction and destination—you're like someone on a scavenger hunt without a list.

Now I'm going to confess that defining a purpose and setting goals is not something that comes easily to me. I fail to get started because I get distracted easily. "Hello. My name is Stephanie, and I'm a procrastinator." It's so easy for me to go chasing after the next fun, shiny thing I see. Sitting down and setting goals for my life is just not something that comes naturally to me. (Why is it so hard to do the very things we know are good for us?) But I can tell you that it's definitely a key to my success. Because a happy life doesn't just happen. We create it with our attitude and actions.

> A HAPPY LIFE DOESN'T JUST HAPPEN. WE CREATE IT WITH OUR ATTITUDE AND ACTIONS.

Authenticity is always a priority for me, so when I talk about my purpose, these are my real stories and my real goals for myself. For example, I have always dreamed of living by the beach where I can look out the window and see the ocean, smell the salty air, and walk down to the shore to stick my toes in the sand and water. And guess where I live now? At the beach! It's my dream come true. Sometimes I still find myself in a state of disbelief and gratitude. So what made this possible? *Blessings, hard work, and planning.* Planning to achieve my purpose and setting very specific goals—with a definite timeline—to reach my success. I was passionate but flexible, and I started to reach the goals I had set for myself.

I achieved what I set out to achieve. And you can too. I want to encourage you to step outside your comfort zone. Stretch yourself. If you really want something, go for it. You just might make your dreams come true.

PLANNING FOR HAPPINESS: THE POWER OF GOAL SETTING

Setting goals may seem a little daunting at first. But I fully believe goals are necessary for success. And don't worry. I'm going to walk you step-by-step through the process. I promise you that I'm going to make it easy for you. You can do this.

Everyone has their own personal goals. I'm using my actual goals for an example, but you do you. Don't do me.

Step 1: Brainstorm

Grab a piece of paper. At the top, write your two mission statements from the previous chapter so you'll have them fresh in your thoughts. Underneath write down any goal or intention you have. Think big-picture goals for the next month, the next year, or for your life. Anything you want. They don't have to be neat, in a list, or in order. This is not the time to edit. Just brainstorm. Write *everything* down. Here's my brainstorm of goals for the next year:

➤ focus on health and wellness
➤ organize work space

➤ watch less television

➤ continue home decorating

➤ organize photo archive system

➤ stay current on memory planner

➤ plan for retirement

➤ travel

➤ take more videos

You'll see that there are more goals here than I can possibly accomplish in a few months, but that's okay. Right now I'm just writing everything down.

Step 2: Pick Three

Now you've got this big list—and I do hope that it's really big and ambitious and filled with stuff that excites and motivates you. Take a look at your list and begin to narrow your focus.

Decide on three things that you most want to focus on. Take your time. Think it over for a day or two if you want. Really focus in on what it is you most want to accomplish. Why? Because if we are focusing on too many things, it's easy to get distracted. Distraction leads to discouragement, which is the complete opposite of what we're trying to do. Here are my three things:

Stephanie's Top 3 Goals

1. focus on health and wellness
2. watch less television
3. organize photo archive system

My Top 3 Goals

1.

2.

3.

DON'T JUST DREAM YOUR DREAMS. CHASE THEM DOWN AND LIVE THEM!

Step 3: Choose a Primary and Secondary Goal

Now that you have your top three goals, I want you to narrow those down even further. Choose one primary goal that will be your main focus. And then choose one secondary goal as well.

For me, my primary goal is to get healthy. Now there are other things on my list that I also want to focus on, but getting healthy is my number one goal. That's where the majority of my effort is going to be focused.

My secondary goal is to watch less television. Let's face it: the hours I spend lounging on the couch binge-watching reality TV could be spent in a more useful way.

As you consider what your primary and secondary goals will be, I want you to dream big; but there are a few things I also want you to keep in mind. Be sure to set goals that meet these criteria:

1. Specific

Your main goal might not be specific yet, but make sure it's one that you can make specific. For example, my goal is to get healthy. That's pretty broad, and it can mean a lot of things. But it's possible to break it down and make it specific. A goal of "be happy" isn't going to work. It's just too broad. Make sure your goal is one that can be made specific.

2. Measurable

You must be able to measure your goal in some way. For example, don't simply say you want to save money. Give yourself a measurable goal like "I want to save $1,000."

3. Attainable

Dream big, but also be realistic. You might say, "I want to be a doctor." If that's an attainable goal for you, go for it! But if you faint at the sight of

a skinned knee, or if the thought of years of medical school makes you queasy, perhaps you should rethink that goal. Set your goals high, but don't discourage yourself by setting a goal that is not attainable.

4. Relevant and Rewarding

Your goal should be something that is motivating to you at this moment, right now. It should also be something that's going to help you achieve your bigger goals of what you want your life to look like five, ten, fifty years down the road. Our world creates this image of perfection and tells you that's what you should shoot for—and it makes you feel "less-than" if you don't achieve it. But you don't have to achieve it. You don't even have to want it. Decide what's important to you, and go for it!

5. Time Specific

Make sure your goal has a deadline. For those of us who are procrastinators, that deadline is key. For example, "I want to save $1,000 by the end of the year."

Now it's time to make the decision: choose your primary and secondary goals. Then you're going to write them down, because that's part of the process. Why? Because when you write down a goal, it becomes more than a wish or a dream; it becomes a promise to yourself.

WHEN YOU WRITE DOWN A GOAL, IT BECOMES MORE THAN A WISH OR A DREAM; IT BECOMES A PROMISE TO YOURSELF.

THINK ON THIS

My Primary Goal

_____

_____

My Secondary Goal

_____

_____

This life isn't going to be handed to you on a silver platter. You've got to go out and get it. But in order to do that, you've got to know what "it" is for you.

Twenty years ago, our entire business was in my garage. My mom and I worked day and night, and we did every job ourselves. We did things that scared us, and there were so many unknowns. But we kept dreaming and going, building and investing. We kept setting goals and working to achieve them. It wasn't easy, and there were times when we failed miserably. When that happened, we didn't quit; we learned and we moved forward. Your dreams, your purpose, your goals are just as attainable. Be willing to do the work, and whatever happens, you will be a success story!

plan a happy life™

JUNE GOALS

*1 Focus on making a HEALTHY shift!
- ⊛ Drink more water
- ⊛ Walk ... Walk ... Walk
- ⊛ Get good quality sleep!

*2 Walk on the beach at least once a week!
- ⊛ Schedule it in my Happy Planner
- ⊛ Soak in the healing ocean air

*3 Finish backyard & plan a 4th of July pool party!
- ⊛ Start a project sheet for party planning
- ⊛ Make a list of action items to complete yard ... and do it!

*4 Schedule DATE NIGHT once a week!
- ⊛ get it scheduled every Sunday
- ⊛ alternate weeks ... His choice — Her choice

5 Develop a workflow for my memory planner
- ⊛ create a system & stick w/ it for the month
- ⊛ Evaluate system @ the end of the month

CHAPTER 5

planning

Plans are dreams in the making.

With our goals in mind, it's now time to create a plan to make those goals our new reality. Because a goal without a plan isn't going to change a thing. And by a plan, I mean really thinking about the action items, the actual step-by-step things we must do to reach our goals. This is a step a lot of people forget or skip, or perhaps they just don't know how to do it. But I promise you this is where the change begins.

BEFORE THE PLANNING

Before we get into the how-to of creating an action plan, let's first go over a few things to keep in mind.

Change Is Coming

As we begin to move forward toward our goals, we are going to encounter change. It's a necessary part of the process. If there were no change, everything would stay exactly the same—which is exactly what we don't want.

Change is a curious thing, though. Many people seem to fear it, and yet change is one of the few things we can be certain will happen in our lives. Over and over and over again. If we can adjust the way we think about change, we can open ourselves to the good that can come with it.

For example, I want to adopt a healthier lifestyle so I can further improve my health and well-being. Can you guess what's coming next? *Change!* I have to actually move my body and become more physically active. If I greet this change with resistance or fear, I'm going to be stuck. Stuck in the same patterns that have gotten me where I am today. If, however, I choose to see this change as an exciting opportunity, one I am thankful for, my whole outlook is transformed and I'm able to see change as a vehicle to grow and learn and thrive. Don't let the fear of change keep you from reaching for your happy life.

> DON'T LET THE FEAR OF CHANGE KEEP YOU FROM REACHING FOR YOUR HAPPY LIFE.

Planning Isn't Always Pretty

I love stickers and washi tape, being creative, and making everything neat and pretty, but the planning process isn't always pretty. And it doesn't have to be. It just needs to happen in a way that works for you.

Here's an example: I like to lay out my plan

for the week on Sundays. I prioritize the action items on my to-do list, decide when I will exercise, and make sure I plan time for self-care and a date night. On Sunday, everything is proactively planned to set me up for success for the week. Some weeks everything goes perfectly according to plan. On other weeks, it rains when I wanted to go walking, or I get sick, or a business dinner gets scheduled for the night I planned to take a relaxing bath. Life happens, and we have to learn to roll with it.

Once upon a time, I wrote my plans (like when to work out) on sticky notes and stuck them in my planner so I could easily rearrange as I needed to. The problem was that I found it all too easy to "rearrange" things right off my calendar, and then they never got done. Now I write my plans in ink—yes, ink! Why? I've found that when I write in ink, I feel that I've made a commit-ment to myself. If life happens and I'm not able to get that workout in on the day I had planned, a sassy little sticker covers that ink right up!

Write It Down!

Organization does not come naturally to me. Being in the planner business, I use a daily planner to keep me on track. I've learned that using a planner increases my

WHEN I TAKE THE TIME ON SUNDAYS TO MAP OUT MY PLAN FOR A SUCCESSFUL WEEK, I *welcome Mondays* INSTEAD OF DREADING THEM.

Stephanie

productivity so I can live a happy life. It allows me to combine my love for creativity with my need for organization. But it was a learned behavior. Now it's a *loved* behavior because it helps me organize my creative, scattered, right-brained world and busy life without sacrificing the creativity and design elements that are so important to me.

Having said that, you use what works for you. Maybe it is a planner, maybe it's a wall calendar on the fridge, or perhaps it's something else. For me, my planner is where I write everything down that has to be done (again, in ink!). When an action item pops into my head, I either write it down on the day it needs to be done, or I jot it down on a "back burner" list I keep on a separate page of my planner. When I write things down, they don't take up space in my mind. I can focus on what I need to be doing in that moment instead of trying to remember all the other things I still need to do.

LET'S GET PLANNING

To create an action-oriented plan, I like to begin by asking myself, "How am I going to make these goals a reality? What do I need to do, and when do I need to do it in order to achieve my goals?" I write those ideas down, and then I follow these steps.

Step 1: Decide on the Details

Dream big, but decide on the details of your plan one month at a time. Trying to plan out your days for longer than that can get you bogged down, and it can backfire on you. When I first started my wellness journey, I spent hours planning out everything for the next year. Three weeks into that plan, I realized it wasn't working for me, and I needed to make changes. Trust me, just plan a month at a time.

Next, break that monthly plan down into weekly and then daily actionable items. You're just brainstorming right now. Grab a piece of paper and jot down anything you can do to help you reach your goal.

For me, my primary goal is to get healthy. That's a really general goal. So first, I'm going to make it more specific by saying I want to lower my cholesterol, improve my cardiovascular health, and manage my stress levels. Then I break those down further to measurable goals like lowering my cholesterol to 120, running a mile, and meditating every day. Next, I brainstorm ways to help me meet those goals.

➤ Walk/jog five days a week—start with thirty minutes, then increase time and speed.
➤ Eat fewer processed foods and less sugar.
➤ Meditate at least five minutes every day.
➤ Drink more water.
➤ Sleep seven to eight hours a night.
➤ Meal prep lunches and dinners in advance.

These are all actionable items I can track. I also know that some of these are my weaknesses, like meal prep. I don't enjoy it, but I know it's key. Lunches and dinners are a pitfall for me, so I need to plan to overcome them. If you know where your weaknesses are or where you will be challenged, you can create a plan ahead of time to overcome that obstacle.

Step 2: Create a System

Set yourself up for success. Set smaller monthly and weekly goals to help you reach your primary goal. Take the ideas you believe will work best for you, write them down, and create a system to track them. Trust me on this: there is power in putting words on paper. You're making a commitment to yourself not only to follow through but to hold yourself accountable. I like to use my planner for tracking, but you can use a journal or an app.

I call my system "Helpful Habits," and I use it to track my progress toward my goal. So, for example, I track my Fitbit totals to see an overview of my activity and sleep totals. And if I'm feeling crafty, I use small stickers to track meditation time and water intake.

I also like to record my emotions and what I'm grateful for. This brings awareness to my behavioral patterns when I feel a certain way. It's been revolutionary in my quest for better overall health. I have found it helpful to include what inspires me and what seems to throw me off track. When we track not only our progress but also our successes, setbacks, and feelings, we're better able to evaluate our plans and make changes where needed.

Step 3: Evaluate

At the end of every week and every month, pause to evaluate your progress. Ask yourself:

➤ How did I do?

➤ What were my victories?

➤ What were my challenges?

➤ What were the things, events, or even people that caused me to stumble?

➤ What were the things, events, or people that encouraged and helped me along the way?

➤ How do I feel about my progress? About the goal itself?

➤ Is the way I'm tracking working for me, or does it need to be tweaked?

➤ What can I do differently in the month ahead to get me closer to my goals?

This is the time to be completely honest with yourself. Look at where you've killed it; see where you've fallen short. Be honest, but also be gentle. Give yourself grace, knowing you're a work in progress. See where your plans have helped you and where they've failed you. Tweak if you need to, and don't feel bad about it. This plan is designed to serve you, not the other way around!

Step 4: Plan Again

Decide on the details of your plan for the next month, making any changes you need to make. Don't be afraid to shift your focus or adjust your goals as your life changes.

It's amazing how doing this simple exercise in planning can help you reach your goals. And when you write it all out it becomes your visual roadmap. That's not to say you won't need to adjust your route occasionally or take a detour. You might even hit a dead end now and then. Remember, planning isn't about perfection; it's about progress. And with a plan in hand, you are on your way!

PLANNING FOR HAPPINESS

As we're planning how to reach our specific goals, it's essential to remember our overarching goal as well: to live a happy life. That means we need to plan to include at least a little happiness and a little creativity in every day. And like anything else, if we don't plan for it, chances are it won't happen.

Planning is not only the key to making our goals a reality; it's also the key to incorporating happiness into our everyday life. Use planning to make sure your days include the little things that refresh and revitalize you, that make you smile.

Take a moment and ask yourself:

➤ What are the little things that make me smile?
➤ What makes me feel renewed and able to take on life's challenges again?
➤ What brings me peace and helps me relax?
➤ What makes my day feel complete?

Maybe it's reading a book or visiting with a friend. Perhaps it's taking a walk in the sunshine alone or with someone you love. Perhaps it's

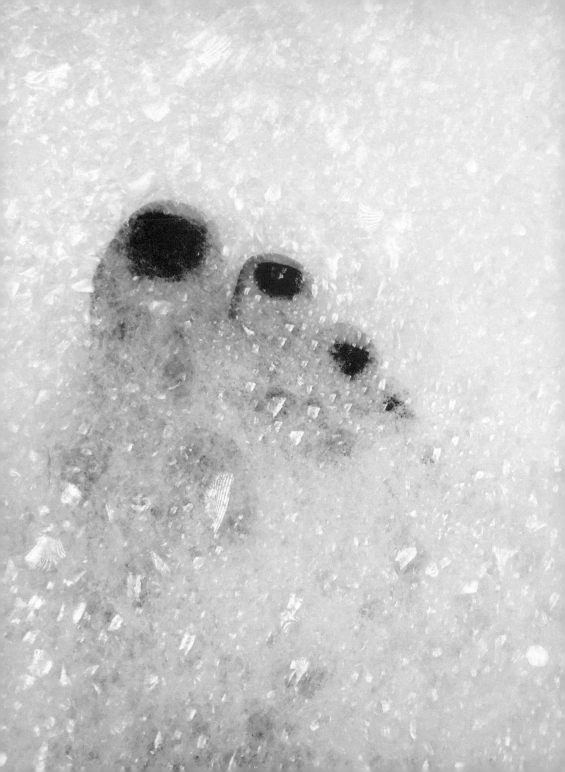

snuggling a child or grandchild. Maybe it's simply taking an evening bubble bath. Or maybe it's tapping into your creativity—painting a picture, cooking a meal, puttering in the garage, or playing with stickers and washi tape. For me, it's creating the time and space in my week to walk barefoot on the beach, belting out some Bruno Mars during my commute, or seeing a movie with my hubby.

Whatever your happy moments are, be sure to include them in your monthly and weekly plans too. Write them in ink as a commitment to yourself. By planning ways to incorporate happiness, joy, and creativity into the everyday, you can embrace a happy life.

THINK ON THIS

What are the little things that bring you joy?

cats,

Put at least one on your calendar each day.

DON'T FAIL TO PLAN

"Failing to plan is planning to fail." That's a bit of wisdom my mom has said to me at least a million times. But she's right. And these words are the reason I know how not only to plan for success but also to plan my way back up onto my feet when I fall. We can't always control what happens in our lives, yet we can control how we react to it and how we move on from it. Here's the plain truth: we are each responsible for our own happiness, and that happiness doesn't happen by accident. To a degree, at least, we can plan for it to happen in our lives. Plan to be happy.

THINK ON THIS

What is a favorite saying or quote you grew up hearing that encourages you to be the best you can be?

_____

_____

_____

A NOTE FROM KRISTIN KELLER, ASSISTANT ART DIRECTOR

Organizing and prioritizing things in my life have always been a struggle for me. I have two girls, Scarlett (seven) and Harper (four), and I'm married to an awesome guy, Jeff. I work full time as a senior graphic designer for me & my BIG ideas. Right now we're in the stage of life where there is always something going on. There's a birthday party on Tuesday; library books are due this week; there's a book fair, so the girls need to bring money to school; we have piano lessons, ballet, Girl Scout meetings, yoga twice a week, and the list goes on and on. This is just a snapshot of what our week typically looks like, and that's just for the girls! Before using the Happy Planner, I'd try to remember things in my head, which I thought would work but obviously didn't. I'd miss things. I'd forget someone's birthday, a playdate, or a fun family event we wanted to attend. Using a planner has helped me become a better mom and a better wife. Now I don't have to worry about remembering all those details, and I am able to manage my time so I have more of it with my family. Not only does it help me be a better mom; it turns into a memory-keeping book of what we did that year and the memories we made.

positivity

Happiness is not just a way you feel;
it's living in a place of gratitude.

While happiness is often the result of planning and creativity, the real choice you're making is *positivity*. Positivity is a state of mind we can choose even when we might not necessarily feel the emotion of happiness. It's important to understand the difference between the two. Let's dive into that a little further.

THE POWER OF POSITIVITY

Positivity is a state of mind we can choose even during the hard and painful times in our lives. We shouldn't choose to just "be happy" and ignore our real emotions. That's not healthy. Processing our feelings is essential for a happy life. But you can choose to train your heart and your mind to focus on what is good in your life, even if all you can think of is that you woke up to live another day. Give thanks for the gift of air in your lungs. Breathe deep and keep going.

Life would be so much simpler if happiness just happened. But it doesn't. We have to be deliberate not only in planning for it but also in seeking it out. That search begins within our own minds and hearts. We have to be intentional about the thoughts we allow to take up space in our minds. Because, yes, we do have control over the way we think about things.

Choosing to approach life with a positive attitude can make all the difference in whether we reach our goal to live a happy life. Our attitudes toward life and our reactions to its challenges are hardwiring our brains for happiness or negativity. That means if we are negative all the time and expect that everything is going to turn out badly, we are hardwiring our brains to believe and expect bad things to happen—and guess what? That's exactly what we will get in our lives. Fortunately, the opposite is also true. By expecting success, blessings, and good things in our lives, we will find them.

Now, I'm not talking about walking through life in some sort of Pollyanna fog of denial. Life can be hard, and bad things do happen. What I am saying is that when we are confronted with a challenge, we need to acknowledge it and then approach it with a positive attitude. We need to be asking ourselves:

Positivity
IS MY
SUPERPOWER.

Stephanie

➤ What is going right?

➤ What can I be thankful for?

➤ What brings me joy? A sense of purpose? Love?

Let's set our sights on these things! They can help us climb the highest mountains and guide us out of the darkest valleys.

It's up to us. We can either sit back and say, "This is terrible! Why does this always happen to me?" Or we can choose to say, "What can I learn from this? How can I move forward?" Choose happiness when you can. Choose to put a positive spin on life's setbacks. Choose to hardwire your brain for positivity, so the happy life you want to live can be yours.

THE GRATITUDE CONNECTION

Maybe you're thinking, *This positivity stuff sounds great, Stephanie, but you don't understand what's happening in my life. How can I be positive in the face of* this *or* that *or* whatever. Oh, friend, I do understand. Because I have been there. No, maybe I haven't lived your exact situation. But I have lived through some really hard experiences, and along the way I've learned some things I hope will help you in your own journey. One of the most important of those lessons is that holding on to a positive and optimistic attitude keeps me moving forward. And I've discovered that the best way to nurture a positive attitude is through gratitude.

Gratitude is one of those things that just changes you, from the inside out. It's what takes your "It always happens to me" mentality and

transforms it into "Wow! I'm learning so much from all these experiences in my life." Gratitude changes you from victim to victor.

So what is gratitude? It's an intentional focus on and acknowledgment of what we have instead of what we lack. And it's *so* important. Yes, I know some of you are going through tough times, and there may be a lot of things going wrong in your life. But even when things aren't going right, there is always something in your life to be thankful for. Even if it is the mere fact that you woke up and have air in your lungs. On the hardest days, that may be all the gratitude you can find, and that's okay.

A GRATEFUL HEART IS A MAGNET FOR MIRACLES.

Practicing gratitude and choosing to see the goodness in our lives train our brains for happiness. There's actual science to back that up. I'm not going to cite it all—and I'm not going to pretend to know how all that works—but trust me, it does! What I do know is that positivity and gratitude have helped me through some of the most difficult times in my life.

Will gratitude make all your pain go away? No. Gratitude isn't going to erase all the hard times; your tears aren't just going to disappear. What gratitude will do is change your heart and mind. It will help you get through to the other side of those tough times—and even find a thing or two to smile about in the midst of them. And if you can take it even deeper, you just might find yourself grateful for the hard times and the changes they've made in you.

THINK ON THIS

Pause for Gratitude

Take a few minutes—whether it's five minutes or thirty minutes—to pause, close your eyes, and focus on the things in your life that you're grateful for. If you're going through a difficult time right now, this might be tougher for you. Just find at least one thing you can be grateful for and hold it close. Let the spirit of gratitude lighten your load and shine a little light into your day.

A LITTLE GRATITUDE CAN GET YOU GOING

Just as a positive outlook is a powerful tool for shaping your life, a grateful heart is a powerful tool for claiming happiness in your life. Combine the two and that power is multiplied, making it a huge motivator to keep you on track to achieve your goals.

GRATITUDE TURNS EVERYTHING YOU HAVE INTO ENOUGH.

For example, here's how that works in my life:

I have to confess that there are times when I just really don't want to work out, even though I know it's good for me and I'll feel better after I do it. To combat this, I have learned to change my attitude to one of positivity and gratitude. I remind myself to be thankful that I am able to exercise, I choose to be happy that I am taking care of my body, and I soon find myself excited to be getting closer to my health and fitness goals. By choosing to focus on the blessings and benefits of working out, I'm motivated to get up and actually do it!

Isn't it incredible how living in gratitude can change everything? Gratitude is so stinking powerful, and it's all in how you choose to think about things and what you choose to focus on. Remember the two key words in that definition: *you* and *choose*. Gratitude is a choice, and it's your choice to make. I know it's not always easy, but I believe that choosing to think positively and focusing on what we have, rather than what we lack, is crucial to claiming our happy lives. A little gratitude goes a long way.

THINK ON THIS

Be a Bliss Seeker

I am a bliss seeker—always on the lookout for things that bring me joy. Sometimes they are big, bold, and obvious, like my family, mambi, and good health. Other times they are small and simple, like a rose blooming in my backyard, someone holding the door open for me, or finding a perfectly ripe avocado. That's not as easy as it sounds! There are days when the good things aren't so easy to see. Some days they even seem invisible, as if they aren't there at all. But I know they are there for me, and they're there for you too. Be a bliss seeker. What are some of the things—big and little—that bring you joy today?

_____

_____

_____

_____

GROWING A GRATEFUL HEART

How can you grow a grateful heart? Plan for it, of course!

Okay, maybe it sounds odd to plan to be grateful. But like anything else we want to bring more of into our lives, we need to plan how to do that. We need to figure out ways to intentionally focus on the goodness in our lives. It's about deciding that we *will* stop and smell the proverbial roses—even in the midst of our busiest and hardest times. Perhaps it's not a full stop but rather a mental pause to notice the goodness and good things in your life and to say, *Thank you*. Here are some tips.

Step 1: What do you want gratitude to look like in your life?

For myself, I want to make sure I am being grateful for this time with my family. I also want to walk through each day noticing things to be grateful for, training my brain and my heart to live in gratitude.

Step 2: What's the plan?

My plan is this:

➤ Wake up in the morning and write down three things I'm grateful for.

➤ Spend my day looking for things that make me happy, that fill up my life. Notice those people and things I'm grateful to be able to experience, have, see, love, and hug.

➤ End the day by writing down three more things I'm grateful for.

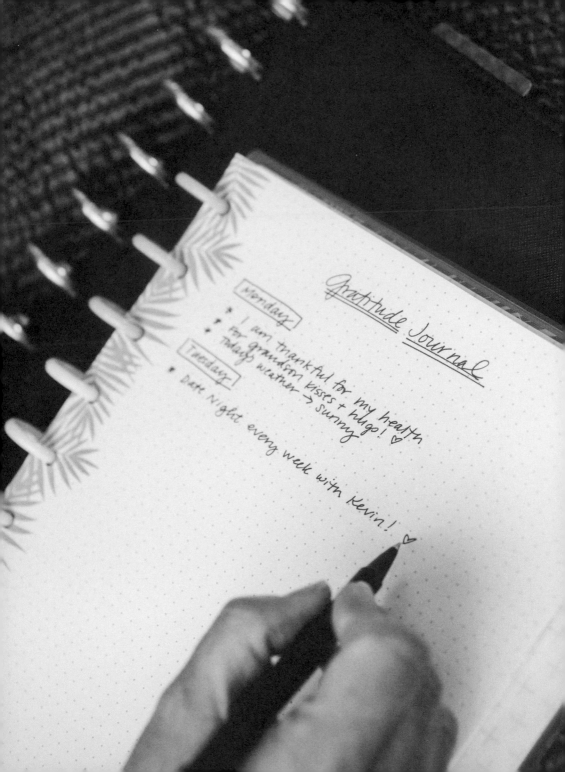

Step 3: Choose a helpful habit.

Notice that I say *helpful* habit. We often use the words *good* and *bad* to describe our habits. But these words can so easily lead to guilt and perfectionism. Let's instead think of it this way: If an action is leading you toward your goal, it's helpful. If it isn't, it's not helpful.

My helpful habit will be writing in a gratitude journal and then pausing to ponder the blessings I've recorded.

Step 4: Pay attention to daily thoughts.

Like any other skill, gratitude is something we need to practice. The decision to see only the things we are lacking, to see only the bad, is a choice and a practice too. Therefore, I will pay attention to how I am walking through each day. Is it noticing the good things or the negative things? I will intentionally guide any negative thoughts back to an attitude of gratitude.

Step 5: Reflect on the week.

At the end of each week, I will write a short note in my gratitude journal, reflecting back and evaluating how well I followed my plan. I will note how it has affected me, as well as other things I may want to focus on.

In our lives, it's so important to remain positive. Collect affirmations and words of encouragement. Treasure them up in your heart and hold on to them. Take them out again to study and sustain you on the days when keeping a positive attitude is so tough.

It's your turn to create your own gratitude plan.

MY GRATEFUL HEART PLAN

Step 1: What do you want gratitude to look like in your life?

_____

_____

_____

_____

Step 2: What's the plan?

_____

_____

_____

_____

Step 3: Choose a helpful habit.

_____

_____

_____

_____

Step 4: Pay attention to daily thoughts.

_____

_____

_____

_____

Step 5: Reflect on the week.

_____

_____

_____

_____

CHAPTER 7

persistence

Good things come to those who hustle.

Persistence. For all the dictionary definitions that can be found, I think perhaps the best definition is the simplest one: just keep going. It speaks to the truth that we have to go after the things that are important to us—things like living a happy life. We have to get out there and work for it. And we have to keep on working on it in the face of obstacles, setbacks, and even failures. If we aren't willing to do that, those wants, wishes, and dreams are not going to become reality.

Whatever it is you want, whatever your definition of happiness is, it's not going to just happen one day. That isn't how life works. You have to take an active role. You've set your goal, you've got your plan, you've determined that you're going to keep a positive attitude and a grateful spirit; now it's time to go out and make it happen.

REDEFINING HUSTLE

I want to start rethinking our definition of hustle. Our culture is caught up in this "gotta do it all, gotta be the best at everything" mentality. I think it's especially hard in today's culture as we try to juggle the responsibilities of career, home, and faith, along with our own personal hopes and dreams.

There's this notion that if you don't do it all, if you're not rising to the top of everything, then you are a failure. Hustle then becomes a representation of all the work, the stuff, and the accomplishments, and those may or may not make you happy.

I just don't believe that's a healthy way to live life. So let's redefine what it means to hustle. Yes, I believe in dreaming big, setting goals, and working really, really hard to achieve them. But let's make sure those goals are what we actually want and not what we think will win the approval of others. What are we hustling for? And what are we sacrificing to get there? We must evaluate the path. Is there room for life, for love, for you? There has to be some room for joy along the way, or what's the point?

> A LITTLE PROGRESS EACH DAY ADDS UP TO BIG RESULTS.

THINK ON THIS

What is a reasonable definition of hustle for your life?

_____

_____

_____

_____

PERSISTENCE PITFALLS

Persistence is the determination to keep going when it isn't easy and when the obstacles are bigger than we ever imagined they could be. It's picking up and carrying on after we've stumbled or fallen flat on our face. And persistence—like so many other things in life—is a decision.

Yes, there will be times in our lives when we have to press Pause— and that's okay! The trouble comes when we allow that Pause to become a Stop or even a Rewind instead of pressing Play and continuing on toward our goals.

What are the pitfalls that keep us from persisting in our quest to reach our goals? We have to be brave enough to look in the mirror, face ourselves, and answer the question of what's really holding us back. I think it all comes down to these three things: the fear of failure, the pressure of perfectionism, and the slow death that comes with procrastination.

Fear of Failure

We set these lofty goals ourselves, and we chart out an amazing plan to make those goals a reality. But then . . . life happens. There's a cold, a cancer, a complication. The deadline is missed. The goal isn't reached. And when that happens, we tend to feel like failures.

We're not failures. *You* are not a failure.

This is so important to understand. You will fall down. You will mess up. It happens to every single one of us. Don't beat yourself up for setbacks. Life is real, people. And sometimes it's hard! Sometimes simply holding your own is a huge victory. Accept that life happens, and then:

- ➤ Pick yourself up and assess what happened.
- ➤ Give yourself some honest feedback—without judgment. You're not a failure or a bad person just because things didn't work out the way you planned.
- ➤ Celebrate your successes. Okay, maybe you didn't write twenty-five pages in your book this week, but you did write ten—and that was more than the week before. So, yay you!
- ➤ Admit your mistakes, and learn from them. Self-awareness is so important!
- ➤ Evaluate and adjust your goals and your plan if you need to.
- ➤ And then *move on.*

Keep going. Persist. You will move past this. I can say this because I'm just like you. In my life, I really want everything to be perfect. And for a long time, when I failed at perfection (and really, who doesn't?), I would just take myself out of the race. Don't do that. Keep running your race. Give yourself permission to be imperfect, even to fail. It's about persistence, not perfection.

So Let's Talk about Perfectionism

Ugh! Can we talk about perfectionism for a minute? Perfectionism is the mean girl, yet we still let her sit at our table and eat lunch with us.

She makes us feel less-than. She encourages us to compare ourselves to others and then shrink into our own insecurities. This whole plan to live a happy life can be decimated by perfectionism.

I have struggled with perfectionism my whole life. But perfectionism is not part of the equation for success. You might think it is, and the world might try to tell you that it is—how many people do you know who wear the "I'm a perfectionist" persona like a badge of honor? For too many years, I was one of them. Perfectionism isn't a badge of honor; it's a shackle that imprisons us.

Perfection isn't attainable, because frankly, it isn't real. If you want to live your happy life, you have got to let the illusion of perfection go.

Perfection will always hold us back. It keeps us feeling less-than and living in our own insecurities. I want you to live in the Four Ps—Purpose, Planning, Positivity, and Persistence—but take perfection out of each one of them. So that thing you thought was your purpose turns out not to be your purpose after all—that's okay! Maybe your plan needs some adjusting, or your attitude could use some work. Perhaps your persistence ebbs and flows on some days. All of that is completely okay. You don't have to be perfect. Just don't give up. Pause, reevaluate, and start again.

Break up with perfectionism. Kick that mean girl to the curb. All she does is drag you further and further away from achieving your goals and claiming your happiness. You will find success when you master persistence, not perfection.

THINK ON THIS

What happiness will you create in your life today?

_____

_____

Get out there today and do something to create happiness in your day and in your life. And don't worry about whether it's perfect!

GIVE IT A TRY

Let's be honest: Do you ever put off writing your name on the first page of your planner or your journal because you feel like it needs to be some sort of modern-day calligraphy masterpiece? That's definitely me! For the longest time, the only opening page that had my name on it was one that I asked an artist friend to write for me! And then, because I knew I couldn't compete with her work, I never wrote my name in other books. But—_news flash!_—we don't have to compete. We don't have to be perfect. We don't even have to be artistic.

So what are you waiting for? Get out your pen and write

your name! Right here, right now! Claim this book as your own. Yes, it might seem trivial. But taking small steps to defeat perfectionism is a powerful thing.

_____

The Slow Death That Comes from Procrastination

Procrastination is right up there with perfectionism and fear of failure when it comes to keeping us from living out the happy life we want to live. It's the slow death of our hopes, dreams, and goals.

Why do we put off happiness? Here's what I say—and I say this to you as your girlfriend and as someone who has lived her whole life procrastinating until I realized how self-sabotaging it was: procrastination comes from two places:

1. We really don't want to do it because it will be hard.
2. We're afraid we won't be perfect or we'll fail completely.

Of course, we don't *say* those things. Instead, we say, "I don't know where to start" or "I don't have all the tools I need yet" or "I'm not sure how to go about it." Procrastination pushes things to tomorrow, next Monday, or that ever-popular, ever-in-the-future January 1.

Don't wait! Don't put off your happy life. Today is the day to start! Where you are right now is your perfect beginning. I know that I'm sometimes guilty of looking at what lies up ahead and thinking it's too big to

THE DEBATE THAT SOMETIMES GOES ON IN MY HEAD CAN BE EPIC. MY INNER CRITIC CAN BE A TOUGH COOKIE WITH A REALLY LOUD VOICE. I REALIZE NOW THAT IF I'M ARGUING WITH MYSELF (OR HER), THAT'S A PRETTY GOOD SIGN THAT I NEED TO GO AHEAD AND DO THAT THING, WHATEVER IT MAY BE. STOP DEBATING AND *just start.* I'M ALWAYS SO GLAD I DID.

Stephanie

conquer or looking behind and beating myself up for what I did wrong. But that's not helpful or healthy. We (including me!) need to move forward with grace, self-love, and a never-quit attitude. There's nothing magical about Monday or January 1. Start where you are and change the ending of your day, your week, your month, your year, your life!

Maybe you're saying, "That sounds great, but, Stephanie, you don't understand how busy my life is right now." Yeah, I do. I really do. Because I've been where you are. And keep in mind that I'm not saying you have to go out and climb the mountain today. Just take the first step, and tomorrow take the next one. A little bit of progress every day will lead you to big results.

If you can let go of those three things—the fear of failure, the pressure of perfectionism, and the slow death that comes from procrastination—if you can notice when they're tripping you up and figure out how to work around them, then you'll be well on your way to reaching your goals and claiming your happy life.

GIVE IT A TRY

What are you waiting for? You know that thing you've been wanting to do? What is it? Write it down here. (Remember, writing it down is like making a promise to yourself.) Now start on it today. Yes, today! Choose one small step to get you going. Sometimes that's all it takes to get the ball rolling.

_____

_____

_____

_____

PERSISTENCE AND THE FOUR Ps

I love the simplicity of the Four Ps:

Purpose + Planning + Positivity + Persistence = A Happy Life

This simple equation really has led not only to my successful business life but, more importantly, to my happy life. And while each of the Ps is important, none of them work without the persistence to see them through.

This equation is simple, but that doesn't mean it's easy to do. There will be times when you don't see any progress and times when you wonder, *What's the point?* Don't give up. Hang in there—*persist*—and put the power of the Four Ps to work in claiming your own happy life.

THE TODAY LIST

Have you ever felt so overwhelmed that you don't even know where to start? Don't worry! You're not alone. And I have a tip that always helps me when the anxiety starts to set in.

Years ago, when I realized I needed to get out of my toxic marriage, I was paralyzed with fear and overwhelmed by all that needed to be done. *Call my attorney (Wait! I don't have an attorney!), find an attorney, sell my house, find a new place to live, figure out custody, research schools, and protect my business.*

The list was huge and scary, and it whirled around and around in my head until I couldn't think straight. It was so overwhelming that I just shut down and didn't do anything. That's when my brother introduced me to this simple and oh-so-effective method: the Today List. It took all that "stuff" spinning around in my head and pulled it into an actionable and prioritized list of what I needed to do. The next time you're overwhelmed by all you need to do—or you simply want to put some order in your schedule—give this a try.

Step 1: Write Everything Down

All of it. Everything that is rolling around in your head. All those things that you've maybe jotted on napkins or random scraps of paper—gather everything up and write it all down in one place.

Step 2: Make a Today List

This is a list of everything that has to happen *today*. Not tomorrow. Not next week. Not next month. Just today.

For me, during those difficult days, it was:

➤ Get up.

➤ Take a shower.

➤ Get the kids off to school.

➤ Go to work.

➤ Get the name of an attorney.

➤ Make dinner.

➤ Spend time with kids.

➤ Go to sleep.

The next day I would change "Get the name of an attorney" to "Call attorney." When I checked that off, I would add something else for the next day.

Step 3: Do the Things on Your Today List

Check them off, and when you've reached the end, know that you've had a good and productive day. Don't beat yourself up for all those other things you didn't do. Focus on what you accomplished and know that you have a plan to deal with the rest.

Write it down. Chart it out. Check it off. So simple yet so effective!

WHEN YOU'RE FEELING OUT OF CONTROL, SCARED, OR NERVOUS, CAPTURE IT ON *paper*. BECAUSE IF ONE PIECE OF YOUR LIFE FEELS OUT OF CONTROL, IT CAN THROW EVERYTHING INTO CHAOS. THEN SET ONE SMALL GOAL. BY BRINGING ORDER TO THIS ONE CORNER OF YOUR LIFE, IT WILL SPILL OVER INTO OTHER PLACES.

PERSONALLY, I LIKE TO USE MY *planner* FOR THIS. MAYBE YOU USE A SIMPLE CALENDAR, A BULLET JOURNAL, OR JUST A LEGAL PAD. USE PAPER TO CREATE A PLAN OF ACTION, TO GET THE LIFE YOU WANT TO HAVE, TO BE THE PERSON YOU WANT TO BE. PAPER IS A TOOL YOU CAN USE TO *move forward* IN YOUR LIFE.

Stephanie

PART III

NURTURING HAPPINESS

Give much. GATHER OFTEN. GREET MANY.

happily inspired

Inspiration can be found everywhere.
You just have to look for it!

I want to encourage everyone to pursue a happy life. It's my mission. I believe it's not only important to fill our lives with the things that make us smile; it's essential to our well-being. But I'd also like to encourage you to dig a little deeper and fill your life—*build* your life—with joy.

THE JOY CONNECTION

Let's talk about joy. *Joy* is a word we are all familiar with, but do we really understand what it is? And how does it differ from happiness? Here's how I differentiate the two:

➤ *Happiness* is what we see happening on the outside. It's when all the positivity within us spills out into our lives.

➤ *Joy* is more profound. It's what's happening on the inside—the internal feelings of purpose, gratitude, and peace. Joy is the foundation of happiness. It's what sustains us and helps us find happiness even in the midst of struggles.

Seek out, nurture, and share those things that bring sustaining joy to your soul. Because that will bring you to a whole new level of living a happy life.

Finding Joy

How do you find your joy? Start by looking at those things that fill your soul with a sense of love, peace, and purpose. Perhaps it's your faith, or your family and friendships, or serving and helping others. Chances are it won't be just one thing.

Joy shows up in my life as delight. It's in spending time with my family, in connecting with people on a deep and personal level, and in nurturing my spiritual life.

I also find joy in the act of creating. When I start a new project, when I allow myself the time and space to explore my ideas, I feel connected to my purpose and talents. Creativity brings joy into my life in the broadest sense of the word.

THINK ON THIS

Where do you find joy?

_____

_____

What things fill you with a deep sense of wonder? Of purpose?

_____

_____

How can you incorporate at least one of these things into your life every day?

_____

_____

How does faith play a role in your joy?

_____

_____

What did you do today to add to your joy?

_____

_____

Look for joy not only in the big things but also in the tiny details of daily life. And take time to document them. Don't keep constantly rushing on to the next thing; let yourself linger in the things that bring joy to your heart. When we open our eyes to the joy inherent in our everyday lives, we begin cultivating a life filled with purpose and significance.

GIVE IT A TRY

Find joy in

- ➤ watching a sunrise or sunset and meditating on the One who created it
- ➤ helping someone
- ➤ being still with your own thoughts
- ➤ taking time to linger and savor the blessings found in each day

Joy ISN'T A DESTINATION YOU SUDDENLY ARRIVE AT ONE DAY. IT'S A *journey* OF COLLECTING MOMENTS ALL ALONG LIFE'S WAY. AND IT'S A JOURNEY YOU HAVE TO DECIDE TO EMBARK ON.

Stephanie

INSPIRED BY OTHERS

I have learned so much from other people, but one of the people I've learned the most from is my mom. She has taught me so many life lessons, like how to

- ➤ dream big
- ➤ nurture my own creativity
- ➤ take chances
- ➤ make a home filled with love and memories
- ➤ be resilient
- ➤ move on from heartbreak

She is bold and brave, and because of her, I know I can be too. These things are precious gifts she has given me. And they're the gifts I want to pass along—not just to my children and grandchildren but also to you. Do you have a person like this in your life? I hope you do. But even if you don't, remember this powerful truth: you can be that person for those around you.

When we support and lift up each other, incredible things happen.

Who has inspired you, and what did they teach you?

_____

_____

_____

_____

_____

How can you pass that inspiration along to others?

_____

_____

_____

_____

Is there something in your own life that inspires you to be a better person? How?

_____

_____

_____

_____

_____

A NOTE FROM JANNA WILSON, SENIOR GRAPHIC DESIGNER

I thrive in joy when I'm intentional about connecting in real life. I notice that when I focus on serving and being aware of others' needs, I find the most joy and energy in my own space. My joy is all about life's *connections* and taking these opportunities to cultivate friendships and encourage others in any way I can. I went through a season of many years of swirling in my own cesspool, too focused on myself and stuck inside myself. But I learned that being both spontaneous and intentional about taking my eyes off myself and reaching out and looking at where I can encourage and lift up others brings the most goodness back to me. Not that I do this well all the time, but this is the truth I preach to myself when I'm down.

INSPIRED TO GIVE

When our own lives are full of joy and happiness, it's easy to be inspired to give of our blessings. Did you know the inverse is also true? Giving of our blessings can inspire joy and happiness in us, even—or perhaps especially—when we aren't feeling particularly joyful or happy.

Because there is more to giving than simply giving out of our material blessings. Enabling and encouraging others to live their own happy lives is a beautiful way to give. And if you are able to do that in a creative way that taps into your talents and also makes you happy, even better! Set a goal for giving, and make a plan to carry it out. Start by asking yourself these questions.

THINK ON THIS

What am I passionate about? Where do I see a need that speaks to my heart?

_____

_____

_____

_____

How can I give in a way that speaks to my passion?

_____

_____

_____

How do I want to make a difference?

_____

_____

_____

How can I use my own personal form of creativity to enrich my giving?

_____

_____

_____

GIVE KINDNESS

PLANT
SMILES.
GROW LAUGHTER.
HARVEST LOVE.

Kind women are the future of womankind. The mambi team came up with this quote to capture the essence of our battle cry. We believe that with kindness to ourselves and others at its core, this saying is powerful! Kindness is not weakness. It's strength through compassion, generosity, and honesty.

There is nothing more powerful than women encouraging and supporting each other! Of all the things I try to do in my life, I hope I will be remembered for being kind. And I hope you will be too.

THINK ON THIS

What are some unexpectedly kind things others have done for me?

_____

_____

_____

_____

What are some simple ways I can be kind?

_____

_____

_____

happy and healthy

Wellness is not a destination; it's a lifelong journey.

I don't believe we can experience all the happiness this life has to offer if we are not actively seeking to live healthier lives. And I don't mean healthy in the strictly physical sense. I mean that we need to be on a wellness journey—one that encompasses our whole lives and that will last until our final day.

I am a product of the '80s diet culture. Yuck! For so long I believed that my health and wellness were tied to my weight, to those numbers on a scale. But wellness is more than reaching your healthy weight or not being sick. It is about paying attention to all the different facets of your life and making sure you are making decisions and taking actions that are helping you be all that you can be.

The wellness journey looks different for everyone. And it's going to change throughout our lives as we grow older (and hopefully wiser), as we go through life's ups and downs, as we change, and as our lives change.

ELEMENTS OF WELLNESS

Wellness is more than what you might think. Being in a state of wellness is not just about the lack of disease or sickness. It's about *thriving* and getting the most out of life by taking care of ourselves physically, mentally, emotionally, and spiritually.

GIVE YOURSELF GRACE.

In recent years, I have had the pleasure of consulting with a wonderful doctor who specializes in integrative medicine. I didn't know what to expect on my first visit. His nurse ushered me to the typical room where I had all my vitals measured. I was then escorted to his office where he greeted me with a warm smile and a gentle gaze. He introduced himself and then asked me, "So, tell me, how are you?" I immediately started going over all my minor health concerns, making sure to be very thorough so we could get to the bottom of my ailments in the allotted time. "No," he said. "Tell me about your life. How is your life? Do you experience joy and love? Are you getting enough sleep? How are *you*?" And, right on cue, I began to cry. Tears of happiness and of relief. I felt seen as a whole human being.

He cared and was going to be a partner in my health, not a treater of my sicknesses. Can I get an amen?

This way of understanding whole-life wellness has radically changed the way I care for myself. When I got home, I scoured the bookstore and internet for all I could find on the subject of wellness. You probably won't be surprised to know that I found a myriad of opinions, but one thing was consistent in my investigation: experts agreed that there are multiple elements or dimensions of wellness. Some cite five, others as many as nine.

Physical

This is what most people think about when they hear the word *wellness*. Things like nourishing our bodies with real food, getting plenty of rest, and moving every day are important elements of living a healthy and happy life. If we don't take care of our physical health, many other areas of our life can suffer. When reviewing your physical wellness, it helps to ask yourself how you feel rather than how you look. Practice shifting your focus from appearance to health.

Emotional

Emotional wellness is being aware of and being able to manage the whole scope of your feelings, from happiness to anger, from stress and anxiety to peacefulness and calm. Do you lead your emotions, or do your emotions lead you? Can you express difficult emotions in helpful ways, or is that something you struggle with? Is there one emotion you struggle with more than others?

Spiritual

This side of wellness centers on finding purpose for your life and answering the question, "Why am I here?" For many, spiritual wellness is tied to faith. Create space and time in your life to ponder these questions and to honor your spiritual life.

Creative

Creativity is our ability to make something out of nothing. I believe we are all born creative, but then, for many of us, something happens, and that creativity is suppressed. Perhaps it's fear of judgment or the pressure of perfectionism. You don't have to go out and paint the Sistine Chapel. Doodle, dance in the kitchen, sing off-key just because you love to sing. Invent a new product, rewire that lamp—creative wellness is exploring your own creativity and appreciating when others do the same.

Occupational

In your chosen field, are you satisfied, happy, and challenged? Does that career—whether it's in a traditional nine-to-five job, as a volunteer, or as a stay-at-home parent—inspire and enrich your life? Don't spend your whole life working away at something that makes you miserable, or even less than happy. Because you can make changes, even little ones, that will make a big difference.

Social

Do you have a rich, connected social life? Are there people you can trust to help you through tough times when you're feeling weak and vulnerable? Do you have a support system? It doesn't have to be huge; mine isn't. But make sure you have someone you can call when that 2:00 a.m. emergency happens. And are you willing to be that person for others?

INVEST IN YOURSELF.

Financial

You might not think about finances as a part of wellness—unless you have ever had to worry about them. There was a time in my life when I would get physically sick to my stomach when the phone rang, because I was pretty sure it was a bill collector wanting money I didn't have. Being financially well means living within your means, saving, and setting goals for the future.

Intellectual

Never stop learning and trying new things. I feel like I get wiser every year, every decade of my life with every situation, every tough time, every victory I experience. This doesn't have to be formal learning either. I'm all for education, but you don't have to have a master's degree to master life and happiness. Just keep exercising your mind.

Environmental

We live in an amazing and beautiful world. Appreciating the wonder of it and recognizing that we have a responsibility to be its caretakers are signs of environmental wellness.

WHAT DOES WELLNESS LOOK LIKE FOR YOU?

Take a few moments—slip away, if you can—to assess where you are in each of the above areas of wellness. Where are your strengths? What do you need to work on? Write down your honest, nonjudgmental assessments. Celebrate the successes, and do something about your weak spots. Set a goal or two. Even little changes tend to snowball until they become life changes. Remember, if you change nothing, nothing will change.

THINK ON THIS

Physical

Today I am

_____

_____

I want to

_____

_____

Emotional

Today I am

_____

_____

I want to

_____

_____

Spiritual

Today I am

_____

_____

I want to

_____

_____

Creative

Today I am

_____

_____

I want to

_____

_____

Occupational

Today I am

_____

_____

I want to

_____

_____

Social

Today I am

_____

_____

I want to

_____

_____

Financial

Today I am

_____

_____

I want to

_____

_____

Intellectual

Today I am

_____

_____

I want to

_____

_____

Environmental

Today I am

_____

_____

I want to

_____

_____

STEPHANIE'S WELLNESS JOURNEY

When I began my own wellness journey, I set some goals that I thought would lead me to a healthier body and life. They were primarily centered on weight loss because I thought reaching my goal weight would be the ultimate victory. But what I learned as I continued in my journey is that there were a whole lot of other things I needed to address first. Things like stress management, emotional eating, self-discipline, and some unhealthy beliefs about my body.

Weight loss needed to be the result of changing my unhealthy behaviors, not my ultimate goal. Otherwise, it's too easy to see a plateau or a setback in weight loss as a failure. In reality, I was making huge leaps in understanding my relationship with food. Losing weight can be like a Band-Aid when we really need stitches.

Now I am training myself (remember, this is a lifelong journey!) to focus on increasing my joy, happiness, and contentment as well as learning to live a healthier lifestyle. Changing unhealthy behaviors is a slow and steady process, one that requires grace and unconditional love for ourselves. We didn't develop our unhealthy habits overnight, and we can't expect to replace them with new, healthier habits overnight either.

CHANGING UNHEALTHY BEHAVIORS IS A SLOW AND STEADY PROCESS, ONE THAT REQUIRES GRACE AND UNCONDITIONAL LOVE FOR OURSELVES IN THE PROCESS.

THINK ON THIS

Taking care of me matters. Today I will nourish my heart, mind, body, and soul by taking care of all these parts of me:

Heart

_____

_____

_____

_____

Mind

_____

_____

_____

_____

Body

_____

_____

_____

_____

Soul

_____

_____

_____

_____

SETTING OUT ON YOUR OWN
WELLNESS JOURNEY

If, right now, you have identified an element of wellness
that needs some attention, you can change that.
Even if that thing you're struggling with is something you can't fully control, you can focus on
the areas of your life you do have control over.
Maybe it's what you're eating; maybe it's choosing to go for a walk or reach out to a friend. Or
perhaps it's something more internal, like choosing
to approach your struggles with a positive attitude.

> BE GENTLE WITH
> YOURSELF. YOU'RE
> DOING THE BEST YOU
> CAN.

ACCEPTANCE: THE PEN IS RED

Last year I visited a health resort where I met with a behavioral psycholo-
gist. He helped me develop some coping skills for the things in my life I
couldn't control. I've been called a control freak once or twice in my life,
so, as you can imagine, situations I can't control are challenging for me.
That day I learned a powerful lesson about acceptance. The therapist
used a word I knew but a concept that was unfamiliar to me: *acceptance*.
He explained it in a metaphor.

Imagine yourself holding a red pen. No matter how much you wish
that pen was black, it isn't. It won't ever be. You can cry, kick, scream,

deny, or wish it wasn't red, but the truth is, it will always be just that: red. You can't control it and you can't change it.

But you can control your actions. You don't have to write with that red pen. You don't have to pick it up. You can go find a black pen to write with. The red pen won't force you to use it. That choice is yours.

Don't spend another second wishing that the red pen will change to black. Go find yourself a black pen and start writing a new story!

Whether you have a specific problem you want to address or you simply want to live a healthier lifestyle, I would encourage you to begin your wellness journey by using the Four Ps of Purpose, Planning, Positivity, and Persistence. Here's what that might look like.

Step 1: Purpose

Figure out your purpose. What is it that you want to achieve? Perhaps you do want to manage the stress in your life. What can you do to make this happen? Break that down into monthly and weekly goals.

Step 2: Plan

Create a plan for how to reach your goals. Make sure your plan is doable by choosing realistic habits that you can stick with every day. Then create a way to track and journal your progress. For example, if you want to calm your mind, you need to identify what is causing you anxiety or stress. Perhaps making time each day for meditation or prayer will help you find more peace of mind. If so, pick a date, plan for it, and start making progress. The point is to break down the steps needed and get going.

Step 3: Positivity

Nothing helps us keep a positive attitude quite so much as having a plan that actually works for us. So at the beginning or end of each day, take a few moments to assess where you are on your wellness journey by answering these questions:

➤ How am I feeling?

➤ Is there something I need?

➤ What can I do to receive what I need?

It's important to answer these questions honestly and without judgment. Is your plan addressing your needs? Or do you need to make some adjustments? Once you have your answers, determine how to take care of those needs—and give yourself a deadline to do it. I know that if I don't give myself a deadline, the things I need just sort of "float" out there, and I never get around to taking care of what I need. These can be big things, or they can be simple things. Maybe you need some alone time. Figure out how to get that for yourself. Maybe you're feeling sluggish and you know you need to eat better. Make small changes to help you meet your need.

At the end of each week, and again at the end of each month, do a big-picture evaluation of how you're doing. This should be done with 100 percent honesty and zero judgment. Lovingly make any changes that are needed. Not because you were wrong or bad or failed. Make changes because you are growing and learning what works best for you.

On my own journey, because I kept track of my emotions as well as my actions, I was able to honestly assess how I was doing. I could see where I was winning and where I was falling behind. I learned that weight loss no longer needed to be the focus of my wellness journey, because I stopped believing I had to live in a smaller body to feel good about myself. Now I move because I love to dance, and I walk the trails around my home because I love being near the ocean. I don't say no to a cupcake when I really want one just because I "shouldn't." I eat brussels sprouts because I like them. And I leave plenty of white space in my planner so I can rest.

Needing to make adjustments to the plan isn't a negative reflection on who we are; it's simply a reflection of human nature. We do better when we know better.

Step 4: Persistence

Remind yourself often that wellness is a journey, not a destination. As with any journey, there will be roadblocks, detours, potholes, and even crashes. Let me urge you to wrap this whole journey up in a big bow of grace and keep going.

This is about progress, not perfection. You might not see the results as quickly as you think you should—but don't give up! The quest for whole-life wellness is a process, and its positive effects are not always visible right away.

I know that my own wellness journey has been a long one with lots of hills and valleys. I know what it's like to feel disappointed and ashamed when I didn't reach my goals. There were times when I allowed that shame to make me feel unworthy and to keep me from my happy life. But here's where I reign victorious: I never gave up on myself or my goals. And no matter what challenges I face in the future, I will keep going until I reach my goals. And so can you.

GIVE IT A TRY

You are your own best cheerleader. Fill a sticky note pad with encouraging and inspirational notes to yourself and leave them where you'll find them over time—tucked in your planner, in drawers, in your Bible, in your purse, or in your car. Bonus: Do the same for a friend or loved one.

Documenting my wellness journey has been a game changer for me. Of course, I made changes to my diet and my exercise, but it was more the intentional act of documenting and reviewing it that helped me grow as a person and embrace a healthier lifestyle. I found what worked for me!

Have you found what works for you? Maybe the wellness journey you're on revolves more around finances or friendships; perhaps it's career or creativity. Whatever it is, if there is something you want, stop thinking about it. Stop wishing and hoping, and do something to make it happen.

Start where you are right now. Don't wait for Monday or for New Year's resolutions. There is no better time than today to start taking care of your body, mind, and soul. Whatever you are able to do today—no matter how big or small—do it and be proud.

PART IV

LIVING HAPPY

YOU ARE *entirely* UP TO YOU.

CHAPTER 10

balance and boundaries

Learning when to say yes and when to say no
is essential to creating healthy boundaries.

Balance and *boundaries* have become buzzwords in our culture today. But what do these words mean? And what do they look like in the real-world lives of real women? There are plenty of textbook definitions out there, but I think the essence of *balance* boils down to this: managing our time and space so there is room for the things we want to do in the midst of all we have to do. *Boundaries*, then, are the tools we use to create and protect that time and space.

Juggling the demands of a career, family, and our own wellness journey is challenging. The fact is, we can never really achieve a permanent and perfect state of balance. It's more like a seesaw, with the weight of our focus switching from one area to another as life demands our attention. And we have to get comfortable with that because that is the reality of our lives today.

For example, I know there have been times when I have needed to focus on the business. In those times, it's easy to allow my wellness to be neglected a bit. No worries. No judgment. No self-loathing or negative talk. As I was able, I simply shifted some of my time back to taking care of me. It really can be as simple as that.

BALANCE: IT'S A MIND-SET

MAKE TIME AND SPACE FOR THE THINGS THAT MATTER TO YOU.

Don't get caught up in thinking, *Oh, I'm just so busy. I don't have time to do anything about balance in my life.* That's nonsense. And I say that as your girl-friend who has had—and sometimes still has—to weed that nonsense out of my life. We absolutely can do something about the craziness in our lives. If we choose to be all scurried, that's a choice we've made.

Let's own that. But I invite you to join me in making a different choice. Slow things down a little bit, live more intentionally, and make some commitments to yourself.

Am I saying it's going to be easy? Absolutely not. I *am* saying that it's possible, and you are worth the effort it will take. Here's some tips to help you get started.

EVEN THOUGH I THINK I HAVE MY LIFE TOGETHER, IT'S NOT "ALL TIED UP IN PRETTY BOXES WITH PERFECT BOWS." THERE ARE MESSY PARTS I HAVE TO DEAL WITH AT TIMES. BUT I'M AT A PLACE IN MY LIFE WHERE I'M OKAY WITH THE *messy parts*. THEY'RE PART OF WHO I AM. I'M NEVER GOING TO HAVE THE PERFECTLY ORGANIZED AND SPOTLESS HOUSE. AND THAT'S OKAY, BECAUSE I'VE LEARNED TO BE *happy* IN THE HOME I HAVE. THERE'S ONLY SO MUCH OF ME TO GO AROUND, AND I HAVE TO CHOOSE HOW TO SPEND MY TIME SO THAT IT MOST BENEFITS ME AND MINE.

Stephanie

Tip 1: Figure Out Your Nonnegotiables

What is it that you must have in your life in order to feel happy and fulfilled? For me, it's making time to move my body, date night every week with my husband, and touching base often with my kids and grand-kids. Those moments in my life are essential to my happiness. They're the "why" behind everything else I do.

THINK ON THIS

My nonnegotiables

_____

_____

_____

Tip 2: Prioritize

There is only so much of us to go around, so we need to choose where our energy goes. Never doubt that if we don't choose, it will be chosen for us!

Planning a happy life requires prioritizing the things that matter.

Not just fitting them in when or if we happen to have a moment of free time. Schedule those nonnegotiables. Put them in your planner. Whether it's a walk after dinner, date night, or a family picnic, having something to look forward to helps us remember what we're working so hard for and ensures that we practice making ourselves and our loved ones a priority.

Tip 3: Create Space

There's nothing wrong with hustling for what you want or working hard in pursuit of your dreams. I'm all for that! But that mind-set starts to go downhill when we equate having a jam-packed schedule with success. Whether it's business meetings, volunteer work, or activities with the kids, constantly rushing from one thing to the next is draining and can actually cause us to miss out on the very happiness we think we're chasing. Create space in your life and in your planner to breathe, to relax, to savor. Create space for happiness to happen.

CREATE SPACE FOR HAPPINESS TO HAPPEN.

Tip 4: Give Yourself Grace

We all get out of balance from time to time—either because of the necessary demands of one area of our life (an illness, deadlines at work, a difficult season of life) or because we haven't been as intentional with our time as we should be. And as women, we can be so hard on ourselves, beating ourselves up for not being everything to everyone.

Get off the guilt train, and give yourself some grace. Fix what you

YOU *don't* HAVE TO DO

IT ALL, AND YOU MOST

DEFINITELY DON'T HAVE TO

DO IT ALL *perfectly*!

Stephanie

can. Apologize if you need to. Walk back through the process of figuring out, prioritizing, and scheduling your nonnegotiables. Then get on with planning and living your happy life.

SETTING BOUNDARIES

For me, creating and keeping any sort of balance in my life comes down to setting boundaries. That means taking control of my time and activities. The primary way I do this is by planning and making lists. My love for planning isn't about creating more time to work; it's about planning to work smarter so I can spend more time enjoying my life and those I love.

When everything is all laid out in my planner, I can see the boundaries of my time and my commitments. Then, as requests come in for me to do this or that, I can realistically say yes or no. Because, let's face it, we don't have unlimited time. Saying yes to one thing often means saying no to something else. Planning is all about making sure we're saying yes to what matters most to us.

The Power of Making Lists

Some things just have to get done: work things, family things, home things. For me, staying on top of all this requires lists.

Making lists makes me happy and helps me feel organized and centered. Checking things *off* my lists makes me even happier. Without lists and planning, my brain looks something like this:

get creative

What's for dinner?

Read!

grocery

EXERCISE!

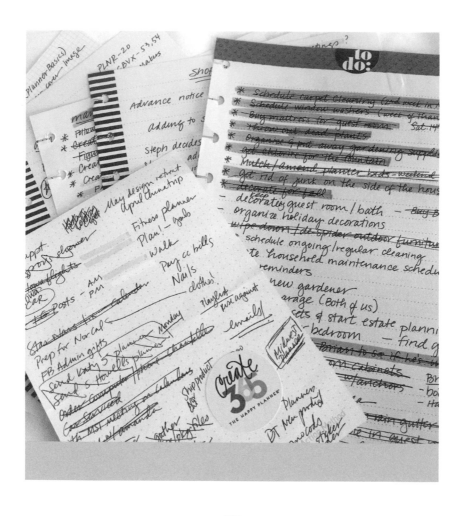

insecurities

laugh ☺

work meeting

sleep

to-do list

vacation

career goals

give back

family time

self-care

laundry

date night

connect with others

call the plumber

Did I unplug the iron?

All the important things start to get lost among the thousands of thoughts constantly popping up in my head. (Can you say, "Squirrel!"?) And forget about prioritizing!

Planning and making lists are essential to my success and peace of mind. Getting all the thoughts and ideas out of my mind and onto paper creates the mental space I need to think big and be present in my life.

The key is to create a system of lists that helps you prioritize, focus, and get stuff done! It's not about glamorizing being busy. It's about being

THE ENEMY OF A FOCUSED MIND IS CLUTTER AND CHAOS.

productive and efficient. It's working smarter, not harder, so you create space in your life for the things and people that really matter to you.

On the following pages, you'll find some practical tools I and others on the Happy Planner team use to create balance and boundaries in our lives. As always, these are tools, not prescriptions. Use what you like and what works for you. Adapt or toss what doesn't. You do you!

A NOTE FROM KAYLA RAHMATULLA, MARKETING COORDINATOR (AND MY DAUGHTER)

Some of the best advice I have ever received is to set boundaries. And to be honest, controlling the boundary bulldozers and toxic people in my life was not that difficult for me. I've always been strong-willed and determined, so standing up to these people wasn't that hard for me to master. What *was* challenging was getting comfortable with saying no to people I love. Events that seemed like fun were hard to pass up.

I have found that when I overcommit, even to good things, I run out of steam and start to feel depleted, maybe even resentful. That's not good. Suddenly, the beauty of a family BBQ isn't as meaningful when what I needed was some alone time and rest. I learned to give myself permission to say no without needing to make an excuse. The truth of "Thank you. I appreciate the invitation, but I really need to rest" is enough.

BUILDING ROUTINES

Routines create habit. Habits are the things we do that we don't really even think about, like brushing our teeth. We can cultivate helpful habits by building and practicing routines in our daily lives. If we continually

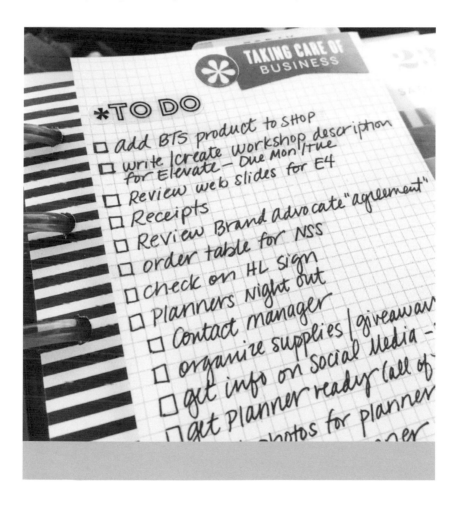

repeat these routines over and over and over, they start to become second nature. Think about what it would be like if you didn't have to find the motivation to go out for a walk; instead, you just did it because that's what you do? How cool would that be?

Routine and self-discipline don't come easy for me. Nope. I haven't mastered these yet, *but* I have experienced great success when I have built and practiced routines in my life. Here are a few of my tips for building helpful routines. (Side note: I'm actually getting inspired just writing this!)

Plan

By now, this shouldn't surprise you. Nothing can take the place of a good plan. Take the time to write down this new routine, then create a plan to make that happen.

Prepare

Good intentions don't make goals a reality. You may have every desire to eat healthier at work, but when lunchtime rolls around and your coworker is heading out for burgers, it makes it much harder to make good choices when you don't have a better option ready to go. Taking the time to prep your lunches the night before can be a key to success if you're trying to eat healthy. That's how preparation sets us up for success.

Just Start

Don't overthink things. And as much as I like to plan things out, don't overplan and underachieve. Just start. You'll fine-tune things as you go.

Find Joy in the Journey

Celebrate the little milestones, and find joy in the journey. You should feel proud of yourself for making positive changes. That's worth celebrating. Yay you!

BEGIN HOW YOU WANT TO END.

Keep Going

If this is something you really want, keep going. New habits take a few weeks to feel normal. Until you get there, keep moving forward.

It's your turn . . . what habit would you like to cultivate?

=== GIVE IT A TRY ===

My Routine to Create a Healthy Habit

_____

_____

_____

22 thursday

23 Friday

24 Saturday

25 Sunday

DECEMBER

Happy Thanksgiving! Started the day w/ a walk along the beach.

I missed these BOYS!!

Be thankful, always.

CHAPTER 11

be present

Life is today, not when you get it together,
when you have it all figured out, or when
everything is perfect. Live your life now—
right in the middle of all the chaos and
imperfection. Smile, play, laugh, love . . . live!

Do you ever find yourself somewhere—even somewhere you really want to be—and you realize your mind has been wandering? Suddenly you're thinking about *all* the things you have to do. You may as well not even be there at all because you are a million miles away, obsessing about the future or the past. What a waste of a perfectly good moment in time! I do this all the time. *All. The. Time.* And I don't like it. One of my ongoing goals is to focus on being in the moment and to be mindful of what is happening in my life right now, because I don't want to miss a thing.

LIFE IS
RIGHT NOW.
LIVE IT!

In our hustle-and-bustle world, it's way too easy to be three steps ahead of ourselves and miss what's going on around us. If this happens to you, you're not alone. It happens to all of us, and it will keep on happening until we intentionally choose to stop it. So here's the plan— the plan to be present.

PLAN TO BE PRESENT

Tip 1: Slow Down

When we find ourselves going too fast or feeling overwhelmed, we need to slow down and breathe. Take five minutes to bring ourselves back to the present.

There are times I find myself completely knotted up, overwhelmed, a wreck. I call it being "spun." That's when I know it's time for me to step back, slow down, and breathe.

When you're feeling spun, take five minutes to

➤ breathe deeply and meditate on the in and out of your own breaths
➤ silence your mind by pouring out your heart in prayer
➤ sit with soothing music or simply silence

Find what works for you to pull you back to the present. Develop a quick and easy go-to practice that will calm your mind.

I will slow down by

_____

_____

Tip 2: Give Experiences

The next time a birthday, a holiday, or even the next weekend (or random Tuesday!) rolls around, try focusing on giving gifts of experiences rather than material things. Celebrate the day by creating a memory.

For example, I have three little grandsons who are completely obsessed with football. Last Christmas I decided to give them the gift of an experience and take the whole family to watch an NFL game. I wrapped up three little footballs to put under the tree, along with a note telling them about the game. The memories we created that game day will last far longer than the footballs—or any other toy I could have given them.

Giving the gift of an experience helps us get away from all the material stuff in our lives and focus on what is truly important: our relationships with the ones we love. Think about all the times in your life when people have shared themselves with you. How precious are those memories? Give that same gift to the ones you love. These shared experiences can be big things, like an NFL game. Or they can simply be baking cookies or playing with stickers together, taking a walk to watch the sunset, or even cooking a meal together. The *what* you do isn't important; it's the sharing of the experience that matters.

TAKE TIME TODAY TO *be present* IN YOUR LIFE. SMELL ALL THE GOOD SMELLS. FEEL THE *sweetness* OF THE AIR AS YOU BREATHE IT. STOP TO NOTICE AND GREET THE PEOPLE YOU PASS BY. BE PRESENT.

Stephanie

THINK ON THIS

A big experience I would like to share is

_____

_____

_____

Little experiences I can give are

_____

_____

_____

I can share myself with others by

_____

_____

_____

Tip 3: Start a New Tradition—Or Keep Up with an Existing One

When things get really busy and you start thinking about all the things you have to do, it's easy for traditions to get kicked out the back door. At least that's what happens to me. But traditions can be important touchstones in our lives and our memories. So I challenge you to embrace the traditions in your life. (Unless there's one that just really doesn't bring you joy; then feel free to kick it to the curb!)

LIVE IN THE MOMENT!

Start a new tradition, revive an old one, or simply keep up with an existing one. Our traditions often seem to center on holidays and special occasions, but that doesn't have to be the case. Celebrate Fridays by treating yourselves to some fresh french fries. Make Saturday nights family game night, spa night just for you, or date night with your sweetie. Traditions help you focus on the moment and are a gift you give to yourself and everyone around you. Be creative with your traditions!

Tip 4: Just Show Up

It truly is that simple. Just show up for yourself in your own life and for those people who need and want you in their lives. It's not just a gift you can give; it's a privilege. Never let yourself forget what an honor it is to have someone want you to be a part of their life. Respect and treasure that by showing up.

Go to the ballgames, the dance recitals, the art showings. Show up for the promotion parties, the showers, the family dinners. Call the friend, bake the cake, send the card. Just show up in people's lives.

IN MY FAMILY, WHEN THE KIDS WERE LITTLE, WE WOULD GATHER THEM UP ON CHRISTMAS EVE—IN THEIR *jammies*—AND BUNDLE THEM INTO THE CAR. WE WOULD EACH HAVE A LITTLE THERMOS OF MEXICAN *hot chocolate*, AND WE WOULD DRIVE AROUND LOOKING AT ALL THE *Christmas lights.* SO SIMPLE, BUT MY KIDS REMEMBER THOSE TIMES TO THIS DAY.

Stephanie

And show up for yourself. If you're working on your wellness journey—and aren't we all in some way?—show up for yourself. That may mean you need to say no to some things in order to say yes to yourself. That's okay. Make time to do what you need to do to be healthy, happy, and whole.

A NOTE FROM LAUREN SHERWIN, VP OF PRODUCT DEVELOPMENT (AND MY SISTER AND BUSINESS PARTNER)

Becoming a mother has been one of the best experiences of my life. But along with all of the wonders of motherhood came new challenges, responsibilities, and worries. Anxiety is something I have had to deal with most of my life, and now I had to worry for two!

One of the best ways I have found to conquer anxiety, fear, and worry is to focus on the present. I am happiest when I'm living in the moment, present and watching what's really happening in my life. Experiencing it. Living in all the moments . . . the *big* ones, the small ones, the messy ones, and even the sad ones. I don't know about you, but I can do only one thing really well at a time. Don't get me wrong. I can be a master juggler when I need to, but if I'm being honest, none of those things gets my full attention. So even though I can "get things done" like a boss, that's not the kind of parent, wife, or friend I strive to be.

I have learned that joy resides in the present. *Joy!* Think about it. The joy you remember from the past is only a memory because you experienced it in that moment some time ago. The joy you are anticipating hasn't happened yet, so it's only a dream right now. We fill our lives with joy and memories by living in the moment and showing up (with all our attention) for ourselves and those we love.

I work at being present every day. It's something I have to practice because, let's face it, it's really easy to be distracted or to get caught up in worrying about what happened in the past or what will happen in the future. If I find myself in that place, I stop, take a deep breath, and remember where I am and why I'm there, embracing the here and now.

We so often get wrapped up in our own thoughts, in our own fears and anxieties. We worry about what might happen in the future, or we agonize over what has already happened in the past. Choosing to be present in this moment frees us from all that.

Being present is both a skill we can practice and a gift we can give—a gift to ourselves and to those we love. Don't wait for the perfect time or place; just show up. Be present. I promise, you won't regret it.

THINK ON THIS

I sometimes struggle to be present because

_____

_____

I will be present for myself by

_____

_____

I will be present for those I love by

_____

_____

I don't want to miss

_____

CONFESSION: I FOUND MYSELF SITTING IN THE STANDS AT MY GRANDSON'S FOOTBALL GAME AND THINKING ABOUT MY GROCERY LIST. I HAD TO STOP MYSELF AND SAY, *RIGHT NOW, I NEED TO BE WATCHING MY GRANDSON. THAT LITTLE BOY WHO STILL LOOKS UP AND WAVES TO MAKE SURE I'M WATCHING. I NEED TO BE IN THIS MOMENT.* IT'S SO EASY TO SLIP AWAY, BUT IT'S JUST AS EASY TO CALL OURSELVES BACK TO WHERE WE NEED TO BE.

Stephanie

NOVEMBER

SU	M	T	W	TH	F	S
1	2	3	4	5	6	7
8	9	10	11	12	13	14
15	16	17	18	19	20	21
22	23	24	25	26	27	28
29	30					

23 MONDAY

MORNING

8:00 Windows Cleaned

Brian picks up bags to take to Mambi

anna to house - discuss Holiday Party - CHA - shipping

11:30 PERISCOPE Black Friday Deals

IMPORTANT

☑ email Kelly @ NSS (follow up) →

☑ Decide on menu for mambi party

☑ Plan table layout for party

☑ schedule CHA meeting for Dec. 12/16 @ 11:00am

☑ email CHA dats to amanda

☐ review flagged emails & answer

EVENING

☑ water succulents

☑ Organize wine glasses / liquor cab.

24 TUESDAY

MORNING

8:30 walk w/ lauren-RSM lake

☑ Send new HP product to Belinda & Charmaine

☑ Create badge list for CHA

☑ email list to andy

☑ create NSS budget & follow up w/kelly

noted

☑ Create release SCHEDULE
- product desc.
- web graphics
- packaged files/ blow outs

☑ Review CHA rental furniture

☐ mambi party
- invites
- plan decorations
- contest
- supplies • timeline

EVENING

☑ Press linens

☑ Take out serving pieces & wash!

☑ Plan table dec.

☑ wipe down outdoor furniture

25 WEDNESDAY

MORNING

Dad & Judi's ANNIVERSARY

☑ Put note on guest bed: don't change sheets!

☑ add Black Friday kits to SHOP!

☑ add slides w/ Dates!

11:00 Skype w/amanda

DON'T forget

1:30 Special Projects Meeting

☐ Plan newslett schedule / conte

☐ Review Her Car re: future camp

☐ contact ↑

☑ Create list of promo codes be Black Friday

EVENING

☑ Take out ta and chairs

☑ Prepare gu and bathr

☑ Target
- water g
- shower

☑ Laund

IT always SEEMS IMPOSSIBLE until it's DONE

It's a busy week but you can do this! FOCUS! and then RELAX & ENJOY Thanksgiving

Be PRESENT and GRATEFUL!

Wake

CHAPTER 12

Celebrate and savor

Celebrate the good stuff, not just the big stuff.

When you see the word *celebrate*, what do you think of? Parties and balloons and big events? We tend to think of the big stuff, right? Things like birthdays, anniversaries, promotions, and holidays. And while those are all certainly worth celebrating, we shouldn't limit ourselves to celebrating only the big stuff.

CELEBRATE

I believe celebration should be a way of life, and we should try to infuse at least a little bit of it into every day of our lives. Because celebration isn't just about balloons and parties; it's about taking time to notice the good stuff in life—whether it's putting the finishing touch on that huge project, nailing the perfect serve in tennis, pulling together a dinner that even the picky child likes, or just making it to Friday.

Why is it so important to incorporate celebrations into every day? Because you know as well as I do that things go wrong in our lives every single day. From flat tires and hitting every red light when you're running late, to sickness, accidents, and worse. All that not-so-great stuff is so easy for us to see and to get focused in on. But if we approach our days looking for reasons to celebrate—you know, that positivity thing we talked about in chapter 6—then our eyes are opened to notice the good stuff too. Celebration acts as a sort of mental buffer, taking some of the edge off life's tougher moments. Noticing the good things that come our way helps us hold on to the happy in life.

So yes, celebrate the holidays, the birthdays and anniversaries, the promotions, but celebrate the ordinary and everyday too. Don't be afraid to celebrate these things:

Celebrate the Simple Things in Life

Celebration as a way of life isn't about finding an excuse to party all the time, but it is permission to seek out and savor all those joyful (sometimes hidden) moments in everyday life. It's finding reasons to laugh out loud. It's dancing when your favorite song plays, smiling up at the sunshine, and splashing through puddles in the rain. Celebrate the things that make you happy.

Celebrate Yourself

You did it! Whatever "it" is—big or small, extraordinary or everyday—take a moment to enjoy your accomplishment. Allow yourself to get excited. Do a little dance. Jump up and down. Squeal a little. Treat yourself. It's okay to be happy with and for yourself. It's even okay to be a little silly when you celebrate!

> IT'S OKAY TO BE HAPPY WITH AND FOR YOURSELF.

And Celebrate Others

Celebrations are always sweeter when they're shared. Just as we should lift up and encourage one another in tough times, we should celebrate the victories of the good times.

Of course, as with any new habit or way of thinking, choosing celebration as a way of life can take a little planning and practice. Grab a sheet of paper and brainstorm some everyday reasons to celebrate—and ways you can celebrate those big and little victories in life.

SOME THOUGHTS ON THOSE BIG CELEBRATIONS

When it comes to the big celebrations—the holidays, graduations, anniversaries, birthdays, and so on—it's so easy to get caught up in what other people expect you to do. Traditions and expectations are fine, as long as they work for you and yours. If they don't, give yourself permission to ditch the expectations and make up your own traditions.

For example, there's a lady who struggled for years to gather her scattered family together for Christmas. But her children were grown with children of their own, and they were each trying to juggle their own family celebrations with in-laws' celebrations. The holidays were turning into a stress-fest instead of a happy time with family. So this lady decided to scrap the traditional. Now her family gathers for Christmas in July to decorate the pool with twinkle lights, put on their Santa-themed Hawaiian shirts, and have a fabulously relaxing time together. Not only did she eliminate the stress from her own Christmas celebrations, she freed her family of the guilt and pressure of trying to do everything and please everyone.

Be creative! Figure out what works for you and yours. If the style of your celebrations is causing stress to you or your loved ones, change it. Do what brings happiness and peace.

SAVOR LIFE BY MAKING MEMORIES

If we are not intentional about our lives, they will slip by in a blur of to-do lists, meetings, and chores. Don't save your memory making for the big days and holidays. Determine to celebrate life and make memories every day—even on those kickin'-back-on-the-couch days.

THINK ON THIS

Today I will remember

_____

_____

Plan to put a little celebration in every day of your life. Sing out loud, splash in a puddle, laugh with someone you love—these are the simple,

FILL YOUR LIFE WITH ADVENTURES, NOT THINGS. HAVE STORIES TO TELL, NOT STUFF TO SHOW.

everyday things that light up our lives with joy. Savor them as you experience them, but why not also document them? After all, with our smartphones, we've got a camera in our hands practically every moment of the day.

Here's an idea: Take a picture every day for a month recording something that made you smile. At the end of the month, gather them all together in your planner, a photo book, or a picture collage. Then take a moment to savor all the blessings and joys in your life.

THINK ON THIS

Simple things I want to savor:

_____

_____

REMEMBER

Personally, I love to look back through pictures and mementos to remember all the wonderful moments of my life. It just brings me so much joy.

When life gets busy, crazy, and hard, I go back to my pictures and think, *Creating these memories and sharing this life with the ones I love—that's what I'm doing all this for.* That's the purpose behind my own memory keeping—to savor life. And it's such an encouragement to me. But to be able to do that, I had to come up with some sort of system to get those pictures out of the cloud, off my phone, and into something I could hold in my hands.

If you're in the same boat, then let me suggest plugging your memory-keeping dilemma into those Four Ps of Purpose, Planning, Positivity, and Persistence. I'll lay out what that looks like for me, but as I always say, *you do you!*

MEMORY KEEPING AND THE FOUR Ps

With the invention of digital cameras and phone cameras, it's easy to be overrun with pictures. What on earth do we do with all the pictures? Try this.

Step 1: Purpose

What is your purpose? What are your goals? Do you want to document every day, just the milestones, or somewhere in between? I like to use a daily memory planner to document the memories of each day. Or at least most days, not all days—let's keep it real! But this is your life. These are your memories. Decide how you want to savor them.

Step 2: Plan

Now that you know what you want the end product to be, how are you going to get there? Create a plan to work through all your pictures. And don't be afraid to experiment a little. Find a process that works for you; that's what's most important.

I like to jot down details on sticky notes each day and place them in my planner. At the end of the week, I go back and add the photos, ticket stubs, and other bits of memorabilia. I try to stay current. It doesn't always happen, but that's the goal.

You can document as much or as little as you want. Do a little each day or catch up at the end of the week or month. I prefer to wait no longer than a week so I don't miss out on documenting the little details that so often get forgotten as time passes by.

Don't forget to add your journaling. Record all the reasons that made that moment special in your life. I like to journal the tough times as well as the happy times. Don't be afraid to be real. Remembering how you overcame difficult times can be a real motivator to keep going when those hard times circle back around. (And don't they always!) After the journaling, I like to add in my stickers and washi tape because they make me happy.

GIVE IT A TRY

When you have a backlog of pictures and mementos from weeks, months, even years . . . here's how I tackle the backlog.

First, I try to stay on top of current photos. The key word there is *try*. Life happens and busy happens, so give yourself grace! Then, as time allows, I go back and fill in a little at a time. Usually I try to just get the pictures in, and then I'll go back and add a bit of journaling. Don't worry about getting supercreative when you're trying to catch up. Sticky notes are fabulous for quickly jotting notes to yourself until you have time to journal the way you want to. Do what you can, a little at a time, and it will add up.

Step 3: Positivity

Corralling all your pictures into an organized album or system can be overwhelming. Just remember the old saying about how you eat an elephant: one bite at a time! Don't let this become a stressful thing. If it begins to get that way, allow yourself to savor this process of keeping your memories. As you go, remember the story that every picture tells.

Step 4: Persistence

This process can be as easy or as involved as you want it to be. Don't feel pressured to make this more work than it needs to be, unless it's something you really enjoy.

One of the biggest obstacles I see to memory keeping is perfectionism. We can get so bogged down in trying to make sure everything is "just right" that we get paralyzed and never really get anywhere. Let go of

JUST GET STARTED!

HERE'S ONE OF MY FAVORITE MEMORY-KEEPING TIPS: IF YOU DON'T HAVE PHOTOS FOR A TIME OR AN EVENT YOU WANT TO REMEMBER, USE *journaling*, STICKERS, OR MEMORABILIA. OR PERHAPS SIMPLY A *picture* THAT'S REPRESENTATIVE OF THAT TIME OR SEASON.

Stephanie

the Pinterest perfection. Don't be constrained by trying to make your memory keeping look like someone else's. Make it your own. After all, this is about bringing you joy. And always remember, done and recorded is better than perfect and unfinished.

My best piece of advice is to just get started. You'll find your groove and start to see what works for you. The process should be easy and creative. This is supposed to be fun, remember? We all have our own style, and yours will be fabulous!

BIRTHDAYS AND ANNIVERSARIES

Make a list of all the birthdays and anniversaries you need to remember. Keeping a master list will make it easier to transfer from one planner to the next over the years.

January

_____

_____

_____

February

_____

_____

_____

_____

March

_____

_____

_____

_____

_____

_____

April

_____

_____

_____

_____

_____

_____

May

_____

June

July

August

PLAN A *happy* LIFE

September

October

November

_____

_____

_____

_____

_____

_____

December

_____

_____

_____

_____

_____

_____

IMPORTANT DATES TO REMEMBER

January

_____

_____

_____

_____

_____

February

_____

_____

_____

_____

_____

March

_____

_____

_____

_____

_____

April

_____

_____

_____

_____

_____

_____

May

_____

_____

_____

_____

_____

June

_____

_____

July

August

_____

_____

_____

_____

_____

September

_____

_____

_____

_____

_____

October

November

December

▲

MAKING YOUR OWN VISUAL BUCKET LIST

You've no doubt heard of bucket lists—those things you want to do before it's too late. I want to challenge you to consider shorter-term bucket lists—for the season of life you're in, for the season of the year, or even a daily bucket list of things you need to fill up your soul each day. Now is the perfect time to create one. To help you get started, I want to share in more detail how I like to make mine.

Step 1

Decide the time frame for your bucket list. Is it for the spring? Is it for the year? While your children are little? Or is it for your whole life?

Step 2

Decide what items will be on your bucket list. I like adding both big and small adventures. That way, when I'm looking for something to do, I have a lot of options. These can be anything you want, from big trips to simple things you want to do with your family and friends, or for yourself. For example, for my summer bucket list, I want to go kayaking, participate in a color run, take a fishing trip, and even try out a sensory deprivation float tank. (That last one honestly has me a little freaked out, but I want to give it a try!)

Step 3

Create a way to track your bucket list. I like to use the Happy Planner Page Protectors for this (the ones for 2x2 cards), but you can use whatever works for you. I write out each item on my list on a 2x2 piece of cardstock and slide them into the pockets.

Step 4

Find an image that represents that item. You can use a picture, magazine clippings, or an image from Pinterest or a Google search. I just took screenshots and that worked perfectly. Size your images to 2x2 (or whatever size you need) and trim. Because I'm obsessed with stickers, I like to add a few of those. Use your creativity and do it however you want.

Step 5

Put the list where you will see it and be inspired by it. That could be on your refrigerator, on your mirror, or on your desk. I keep mine in my planner so I see it every day.

Step 6

When you check an item off your list, be sure to capture the moment with a photo or selfie. You'll be so glad you did. Add your photo to your bucket list as a lovely reminder of dreams come true.

BUCKET-LIST IDEAS

Monthly

_____

_____

_____

Spring

_____

_____

Summer

_____

_____

Fall

_____

_____

Winter

_____

_____

Lifetime

_____

_____

CONCLUSION

PLAN A HAPPY LIFE

Think happy. Plan happy. Be happy.

To the woman who is about to finish this book, please know that I am just like you. *Real*. I win and I lose. I fall down and I pick myself up again. Just like you.

I'm not a life coach or some sort of self-help expert. I don't pretend to have all the answers. But I do have plenty of experience with life at its best and its worst. This book holds the wisdom and the strategies that have helped me find and claim my own happy life. It's what works for me, and it's very personal. Take what works for you, adapt it, and make it your own. And as you do, I pray that you will

➤ find peace in the midst of life's storms;

➤ learn to truly love and accept yourself for the amazing woman you are;

- ➤ be encouraged to keep going;
- ➤ be inspired to dare for more;
- ➤ and, most of all, know that you have the ability and the power to reach out and claim the happy life you want to live.

It has taken more than twenty years of hard work, planning, and a whole lot of heart to get my company, me & my BIG ideas, to where it is today If you are following your own big ideas, and things aren't happening as quickly as you'd like, keep going. Believe in yourself, plan for success, and work hard for what you want.

Don't be afraid to do something big, knowing that you are the one who gets to define exactly what *big* means to you. In other words, plan your own happy life and then . . . go out and live it!

THE FUTURE BEGINS NOW!

ABOUT THE AUTHOR

Stephanie Fleming is a creative entrepreneur, speaker, optimist, and wellness seeker. Most notably, she is the cofounder of me & my BIG ideas, creators of the Happy Planner. The business that began twenty years ago as a tiny garage-based business is now an industry-leading lifestyle brand that offers a wide variety of products that inspire customers to *Live Creatively®* and *Plan a Happy Life™*.

Stephanie lives happily in her dream-come-true California beach house with her husband (and business partner), Kevin. She has two grown children, two stepchildren, and three amazing grandsons. It is her mission to create a Happy Life Movement by empowering people everywhere to take control of their own happiness by embracing planning, positivity, and all things creative!

For more ideas and inspiration for your happy life, connect with Stephanie at www.thehappyplanner.com or on Instagram @the_happy_planner or @stephanie_fleming.

BONUS
CONTENT

HELLO, HAPPINESS SEEKERS!

You did it! You finished the book and are ready to go out and live your happy life. Give yourself a congratulatory high five. You deserve it. I am so excited to share this bonus content with you because I wholeheartedly believe it can change the way you move forward in your journey of creating a happy life.

Over the years I have used the practice of mind-mapping to brainstorm ideas. These have become my happy maps! This type of brainstorming is a highly effective and fun way to get those ideas out of your head and onto paper. Mind maps (or radial maps) start with one word, question, or concept in the center of the page, and then you add inspiring ideas that branch from the original idea. It's kind of hard to articulate, so take a look at a sample I created for the question "What makes me happy?"

To get started, here's what you do:

➤ Write, "What makes me happy?" in the center box.
➤ Then jot down your answers at the end of the lines that radiate from the center. (I love to use different color pens for this part!)
➤ Once all your lines are filled, choose one branch to focus on and write down everything you can think of that relates to the topic.
➤ Continue with the process until the page is full of happy ideas!

Please don't feel pressured to make it pretty or perfect. The whole point of this exercise is to find your flow and to keep it going. Your inner critic is not invited to this party.

When you have finished, you will have a whole page of things you can do that will make you happier. This exercise helps us expand our ideas into smaller, more specific steps to help us achieve our goals.

I have included some of my favorite prompts to get you started, but you can also use this new skill any time you want to explore an idea or dive a little deeper into a new concept.

Wishing you a lifetime of happiness,

Stephanie

HAP
PIN
ESS

create space for

happiness to happen

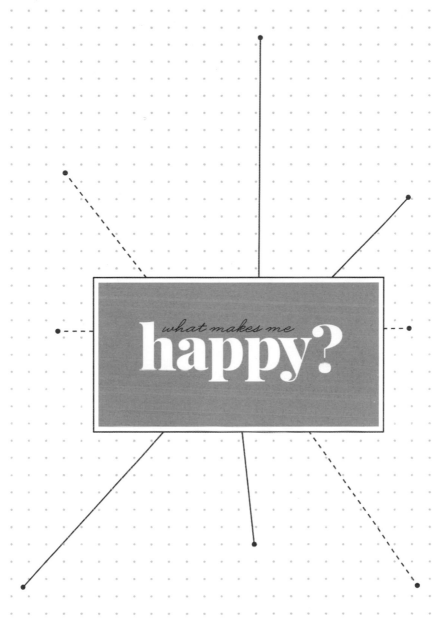

what makes me
happy?

goal
PLAN
EVALUATE

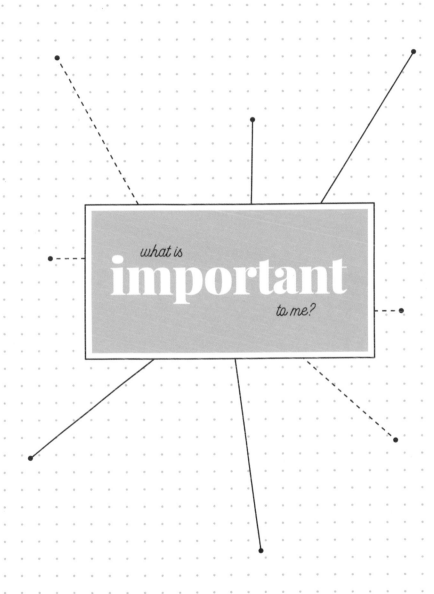

what is
important
to me?

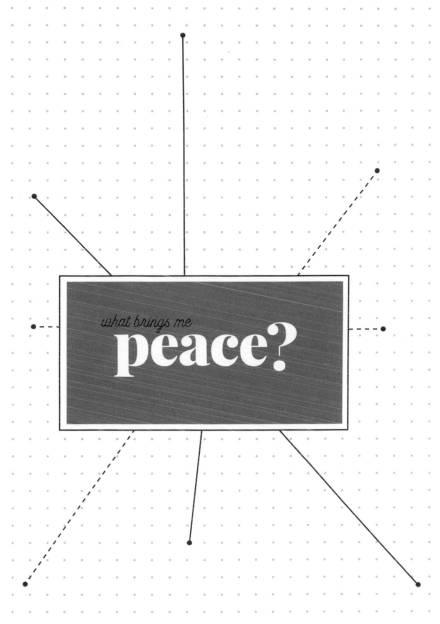

what brings me
peace?

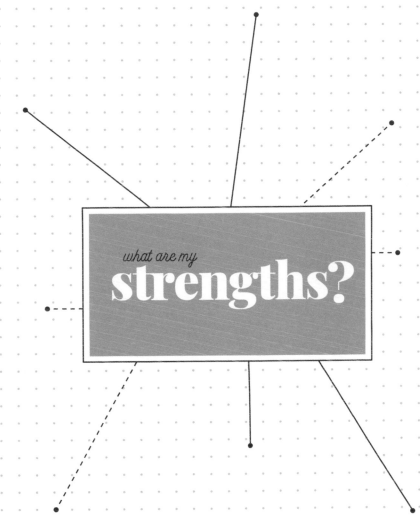

what are my
strengths?

HAPPY TO BE ME

- ♥ I am enough.
- ♥ I am worthy.
- ♥ I am strong.
- ♥ I am beautiful.
- ♥ I am smart.
- ♥ I believe I am ...
- ♥ I deserve ...
- ♥ I want to be ...
- ♥ You do YOU!
- ♥ Real is beautiful, and so am I!

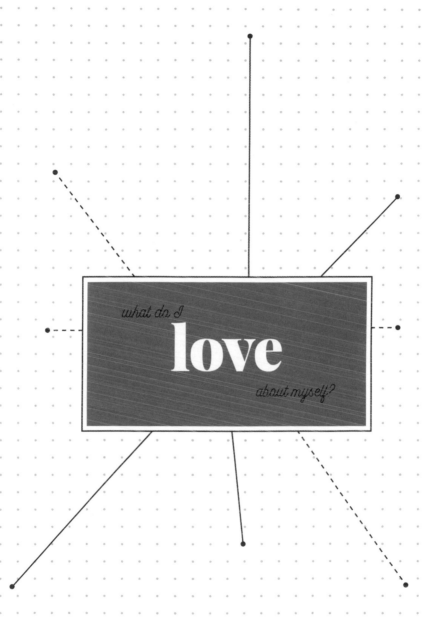

what do I **love** about myself?

life
is
right
now.
live it!

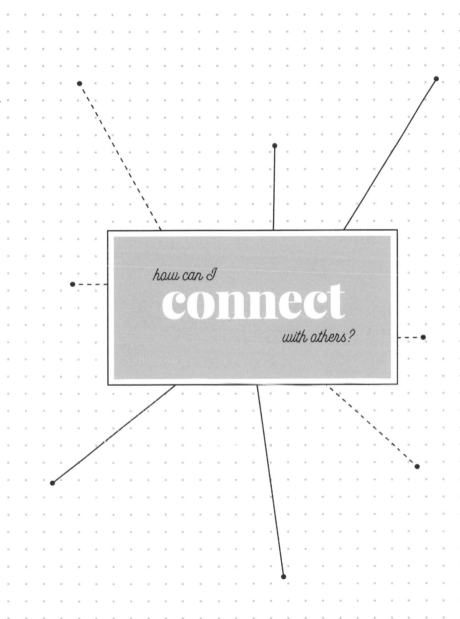

how can I

connect

with others?